100 YEARS ON

The first Bradford City FC, the early years of Bradford (Park Avenue) & other stories

Rob Grillo

Manchester

PARRS WOOD PRESS

THE PARRS WOOD PRESS
St.Wilfrid's Enterprise Centre
Royce Road, Manchester, M15 5BJ

Copyright, Rob Grillo

ISBN: 1 903158 24 9

Produced by Rob Grillo, with the assistance of Andrew Searle of The Parrs Wood Press.

Printed by:
Fretwell Print & Design
Healey Works, Goulbourne Street,
Keighley, W.Yorks,

100 YEARS ON

The first Bradford City FC, the early years of Bradford (Park Avenue) & other stories

Contents

Bradford & Bingley*

BRADFORD CITY FOOTBALL CLUB

FOREWORD

I was fortunate to read a draft copy of Rob Grillo's dedicated work prior to publication.

I believe that it will give much pleasure to everybody who is interested in the history of football in Bradford. A real work of literary importance for the dedicated followers of the sport and also a work of social importance as it gives, in effect, an insight into life in Bradford at the turn of the Century.

I would like therefore, to unreservedly recommend your purchase of this unique book which will give many hours of pleasure.

Geoffrey Richmond,
Chairman.

Bradford City A.F.C. (1983) Ltd. The Bradford & Bingley Stadium, Valley Parade, Bradford, West Yorkshire, BD8 7DY.
Telephone: Bradford (01274) 773355 Facsimile: Bradford (01274) 773356 Ticket office: Bradford (01274) 770022
Commercial Department: Bradford (01274) 778778 Bantams Leisure: Bradford (01274) 770012
e-mail: bradfordcityfc@compuserve.com website: www.bradfordcityfc.co.uk
Club Call No. 09068 - 888640 (calls charged at 60p per minute - all times)
Registered No. 1732784 England

FAMILY SECTION
SPONSOR

STAND SPONSORS

City of Bradford.

Bradford's first coat of arms, granted on 18th October 1847. It was still in use when Bradford FC and Bradford City took to the field in the mid 1890's and early years of the 20th century respectively. Later additions to the coat of arms – the ram & goat supporters– were added on 31st December 1907, while a redesigned coat of arms was inaugurated in 1974 when Bradford became a 'metropolitan district'.

1
INTRODUCTION

In May 1903 Bradford City Football Club was elected to the expanding Football League. League officials were keen to gain a foothold in the woollen region of the West Riding, which had for many years been a rugby stronghold. That City had never played a competitive 'soccer' game mattered little to the powers that be, who had no hesitation in accepting the newly formed soccer club into its ranks in place of Doncaster Rovers.

City's history actually goes further back, to the formation of the Manningham Albion rugby club as early as 1872. Founder members of the Northern Union (Rugby League), minus the 'Albion' tag, and following the 'great split' in 1895, the club moved from their former Carlisle Road base to Valley Parade in 1886. Faced with potentially crippling debts, Manningham took up the round ball game and renamed themselves Bradford City FC in 1903.

However, it is little known that the name of Bradford City had been used before 1903. Little more than what would now be considered a 'parks' team, the original Bradford City club played out the 1901-02 season in the Bradford & District League, coming close to winning two sets of silverware, played one game *away* from home at Valley Parade, and then disappeared as quickly as it had at first appeared. Another, even more obscure side of the same name then played out the 1902-03 campaign, despite Manningham's intention to revert to a club of the same name the following year.

During the course of my research, my attention was drawn towards other local sides of the time – not only those teams competing against the first Bradford City in their one and only season, but more notably in those teams that had preceded City. This brought me to another 'grey' area – that of the early history of Bradford Park Avenue FC.

Most reference books will tell you that the original Park Avenue were formed in 1907 when Bradford FC abandoned Rugby in favour of 'soccer', as Manningham had done just a few years earlier. However, inspired by the few facts regarding Bradford FC's first forays into the round ball game, uncovered by other like-minded sports historians such as Pete Zemroch, I delved further into the depths of history to uncover lost league tables and results from what were essentially Park Avenue's forerunners.

Therefore this is more than just a short study into the early history of Bradford City! It also unravels the formative years of the association game at Park Avenue, as well as looking at the early years of organised soccer in the city as a whole.

To say that sources of information relating to the early years of Bradford (Park Avenue) and the original Bradford City are hard to come by is something of an understatement. Local newspapers of the time often proved sketchy in their coverage of local 'soccer' in a rugby dominated era, and photographs of the teams' home grounds at the time have also proved hard to come by, despite the fact that City's ground later became a home of greyhound racing as well as being used for one season by Bradford Northern RLFC before its demise. In fact, photographs have been virtually impossible to come by; unsurprising when we are looking back to a time when the camera was considered a luxury of the few. I have therefore used old ordnance survey maps to illustrate, as well as original newspaper reports of the time and previously uncovered league tables.

Thanks to (in no particular order):
John Dewhirst & Dave Pendleton (City Gent), Fred H.Hawthorn (3:2 books), Manny Grillo, Trevor Delaney, Pete Zemroch (Bradford Park Avenue), Andy Searle (Parrs Wood Press) & the staff in the reference sections at Bradford and Keighley Libraries.

Copyright owners of the few photographs in this book are unknown, apologies if copyright has been infringed in any way. Baines cards courtesy of John Dewhirst.

2
BRADFORD'S FIRST TASTE OF LEAGUE FOOTBALL

BRADFORD FC 1895-99

The Bradford & District Football Association was formed in March 1899, following a meeting at 'County restaurant'. It was charged with organising the many teams in the area, who had previously played only friendly fixtures against each other, into formalised leagues. Teams with a ground within a six-mile radius of the city centre were invited to join the fledgling association, the entrance fee to which was 10/6d.

The round ball game had certainly taken long enough to take off in the region. Cricket and rugby had already seen a phenomenal growth since the 1850's, mainly due to the 1850 Factories Act which ensured a five and a half day working week for the vast majority of the nations workforce. Now for the first time, aspiring sports stars were able to not only take part in their favourite pastime, but also to watch their local side or favourite stars in action. Gate receipts spiralled as four figure crowds graced the grounds of local cricket and rugby teams and local sport was booming. Further to this, the 'railway boom' of the time saw a new station opened on the Leeds and Bradford Railway at Manningham in 1867, making the rugby ground at Valley Parade much more accessible, followed by a similar opening at Horton Park on the Bradford and Thornton line in 1878, adjacent to what would be the renown Park Avenue sports grounds.

A local Football Association was formed in the nearby Heavy Woollen district twelve months prior to that in Bradford, and the first fixtures of in new Heavy Woollen League played on 24th September 1898 (eventual champions were Saviletown Clarence). It was no surprise then that the aspiring clubs and individuals of Bradford would follow suit soon after.

The city's first flirtation with the Association game had come much earlier than the formation of the local FA though. This occurred when Bradford cricket and rugby clubs merged in 1880. The rugby club had been playing at Apperley Bridge since the mid 1870's, while the cricket club initially played on land which is now covered by Pemberton Drive, opposite the present day University. Their amalgamation co-incided with a move to Park Avenue in 1882, and it is possible that some 'experimental' association fixtures or practices may have been held *. A much more concerted effort to play the round ball game however, saw the club's association section join a twelve team West Yorkshire League for the 1895-96 season. This league had been formed twelve months previously and was the first attempt at serious league competition in the West Riding of Yorkshire.

It is believed that the new soccer section at Park Avenue may have been formed through the wholesale recruitment of Apperley Bridge based side Buckstone Park FC, although no mention was made of this in the local press at the time. Rugby & Soccer were, where possible, played on alternative Saturdays at Park Avenue although at times other grounds within the city boundaries were to be utilized.

Possibly the first fixture to be played in what was the city's first serious attempt at the round ball game was a friendly at Swinton (Rotherham) on 7th September 1895. The local vicar kicked off and from an early stage it was obvious that the home team were a far more superior team, the South Yorkshire side running out winners by three clear goals.
The Bradford side for this first game was:
H.Killick (goal), **I.Smith, H.Collinson** (backs**), R.Thorne, A.Shepherd** *(captain)***, Norman Thorne** (half backs**), C.Ackroyd, C.Ingham** (right wing), **Healey, Laidlaw** (left wing), **J.Miles (**centre), **R.Jenkins, H.Thorne** (reserves),

One week later another 'friendly' fixture was fulfilled, the first home game of the season, against Manchester outfit Moss Side. With several first team members being reported as being on holiday, a number of 'reserves' were called upon. Despite this, a 4-1 victory was achieved – goals from Whyte and Matthews in the first half, and a brace from David Menzies, playing his first game, in the second, ensuring the 3000 or so home spectators left Park Avenue happy.

---

* Other groups also experimented with the game in 19th Century Bradford. September 1888 saw a newly formed side, based at Thornbury, lose 0-2 at home to an early Keighley FC. This 'Bradford' side also lost the return 1-2 two months later (their goal scored by Petrocochins), and it is known that they played other sides from across the county in friendlies. This side played some second team fixtures also, one such match resulting in a 10-0 home success against Keighley 'A'.

West Yorkshire League fixtures resumed in earnest on September 7th, the same date as Bradford's friendly at Swinton, but Bradford still had two more fixtures to fulfill before they commenced their league programme. Ackworth School were defeated 4-3 on their own ground on 21st September, the defeat reportedly being the side's first at home for two seasons. A brace from Lee in the first half, and two further second half strikes – the first following a *melee* in the Ackworth goalmouth and the deciding strike from Laidlaw saw Bradford victorious. The Ackworth players must have impressed however, as Thompson was at least one of their side later to appear in Bradford FC colours later in the season.

Three days later an exhibition match was played at Park Avenue when Football League giants Bolton Wanderers made their first visit to Bradford. It was reported that over 3000 packed the then basic Bradford enclosure (in later years described as being over 5000!) Although this was by far the biggest 'association' game involving a local side, FA cup giants Blackburn Rovers had played a demonstration match there against a Blackburn Olympic (also former FA Cup winners) several years earlier. Bolton won easily by 7 goals to 2, but the loudest cheers were saved for two second half strikes for Bradford by Collinson and Ackroyd.

The first league fixture was at last played on 28th September 1895, when Featherstone were dispatched 4-2 at Park Avenue. Despite strikes from Ingham (2), Ackroyd and Laidlaw, the 'Bradford Observer' was less than complementary about the afternoon's proceedings:
  ' *Both the teams played a fairly good game but there was a notable deficiency in dribbling power, even in some of the more energetic players'*.

The following Saturday saw a visit to Hunslet – and a 1-7 thrashing for the locals at the hands of a side who were already well clear at the head of the league table. Matthews and Menzies then grabbed two each in a 4-0 home defeat of Huddersfield in a friendly match in front of 2000 spectators the following week. This was followed by another home victory – 2-0 against Halifax in what was described in the same newspaper as a *'capital game'* – although there were only an estimated 1000 present for this fixture. Menzies was again on the mark, along with Ingham, and by now H.M.Lemoine was keeping goal for the Bradford side.

October 1985 finished with an easy 8-1 victory for Bradford against Harrogate St.Peters in the 'Leeds Workpeople's Hospital Cup'. This cup, despite its name, was in-fact the strongest knock-out competition in the county and included all West Yorkshire League teams as well as a number of more 'junior' sides. There were only 500 present at Park Avenue for this game, but this was a surprisingly large number when you consider that not far away at Valley Parade, Manningham rugby club were defeating Bradford in a classic local derby by 8 points to 4.

There was no report in the local press of Bradford's next league fixture, at Altofts on 2nd November, although it is believed that the match was lost 1-3. Although Oulton were then defeated 6-3 at home in front of a small crowd, there was at this time no indication that Bradford would be anything other than 'also rans' in the league. The locals lay 7th of the twelve teams at this time, and although the seemingly ever changing team was showing signs of improvement, they were well adrift of runaway leaders Hunslet.

Two more league matches – a 2-0 win at Castleford despite having a '*shaky looking team*' and a 1-1 draw in the return fixture at Featherstone followed, before two farcical games, both of which resulted in victories against strong opposition, yet neither of which yielded league points.

Leeds visited Bradford on November 11th. With Park Avenue unavailable for the first time, a ground at Apperley Bridge was procured. The Bradford Observer bemoaned the fact that this enclosure was not conducive to drawing a good gate, but this was a secondary concern to the fact that despite Bradford winning 6-2 the match was ordered to be replayed by the league committee due to the game kicking off late and 'short time' being played.

The following Saturday brought Hunslet to Park Avenue – or rather Hunslet reserves. Forced to play an English Amateur Cup tie against Hartlepool NER the same day (which they won 3-1), Hunslet sent over their second string and in front of another small attendance a friendly fixture was played – Bradford winning easily, 6-0.

Normanton were then defeated 3-2 away from home on a quagmire of a pitch (at last two points could be claimed!) before yet another friendly fixture, a 4-0 home defeat of Scarborough. As the visitors missed a connecting train, the game again had to be cut short, with two halves of 30 minutes played. By now Menzies, along with one (or more!) of the Thorpe brothers, were in a rich vein of form, and the Monday's local press usually contained details of their by now all-too predictable goalscoring exploits. They were more than likely on target in a victory at Leeds side Oulton, but this fixture – which was definitely won by the Bradford side – has not yet been traced.

Hunslet came to Park Avenue again three days after Christmas, this time for a Leeds Hospital Cup-tie. 1500 spectators witnessed one of the most exciting games of the season as the home side, despite being without captain, Shepherd, won a titanic battle 7-4! There was clear evidence in this result that the locals had made a marked improvement, but following a 4-5 reversal in a league fixture at Halifax's Hanson Lane cricket ground (their first game of 1896) they still lay only 7th in the table. The Bradford Observer stated that despite a fine showing in the first half, Bradford were *'disorganised and spiritless'* in the second! However, the Halifax game proved to be Bradford's last competitive defeat of the season as they embarked on a remarkable series of victories that would see them rise to the top of the league table.

Also at this time, a Bradford *reserve* side was turning out for the occasional fixture, winning 6-2 at Pudsey on 11th January (when lowly Oulton were possibly defeated in that unrecorded fixture) and then drawing 2-2 against Normanton reserves, on the same day that the senior Bradford side were defeating the same opposition 4-0 in front of almost 4000 at Park Avenue. The side was now fifth in the league – Hunslet still top with 11 wins from 12 fixtures.

A ground at Girlington then had to be used for the next fixture – against Pontefract Garrison. Unfortunately despite strenuous efforts to get the game played, the army side turned up late and two halves of 30 minutes again had to be played. At least the soldiers turned up though – the official referee didn't and the 3-0 victory for Bradford was achieved in another 'friendly' encounter. A midweek 6-1 victory was achieved at the ground of the same opposition less than two weeks later – luckily the referee did turn up this time- and sandwiched between this was a 4-0 home success in front of 2000 against Castleford for the in-form Bradford team.

By now Ferrybridge had resigned from the league, this left Bradford with a free date on 8th February, so yet another friendly fixture was played. Yorkshire College, who had a number of Bradford FC players in their side, were the opponents. The Girlington enclosure was again utilized, and again the visitors were defeated, this time 2-1.

What followed was a 2-2 draw at home to Altofts one week later. However, the locals let a two goal half time lead slip. Strikes by A.Thorpe and Menzies were not enough to see off a spirited side who would go on to defeat Hunslet seven days later. However, this was not to be only occasion in which Bradford would let a two goal lead slip before the end of the season – and this would prove crucial to the outcome of their season.

On the same day that leaders Hunslet went down 1-2 to Altofts, Bradford were seeing off Rothwell to the tune of 4-1. Then followed a Leeds Hospital Cup semi-final against Leeds FC at neutral Hanson Lane, Halifax. For the second time a two-goal lead was surrendered by the Bradford side – Ingham and Thompson on target this time – which led to a replay being required. Ironically the other semi-final, between Normanton and Featherstone was played in front of a small attendance at Park Avenue. Normanton won 3-1 but fielded ineligible players, and Featherstone won the replay!

The Bradford-Leeds replay was played at Valley Parade! This means that the Bradford (Park Avenue) club played a fixture at Valley Parade before any Bradford City side did! On this occasion, a two-goal lead was not surrendered – 3000 spectators witnessing a convincing 4-0 Bradford victory.

Seven days later, Leeds returned to Bradford – this time to Apperley Bridge again to replay their earlier league fixture. Bradford won a much tighter game 2-1 this time.

In between the two semi-final ties, Bradford had achieved a convincing 9-0 victory in the 'replayed' home fixture against Pontefract Garrison in front of 2000 elated Park Avenue supporters. This was not the home side's biggest victory as the season however, as 10-man Rothwell, struggling at the foot of the table, were annihilated 13-0 at the same ground at the end of March. Reginald Thorne found the net no less than six times in the game, followed by David Menzies, who hit four.

April proved a busy – and crucial - period for Bradford FC. A visit to Scarborough in a friendly on April 4th resulted in a 3-6 loss, before the Leeds Hospital Cup final tie against Featherstone two days later (Easter Monday). There were between 2000 & 3000 spectators at the neutral Hunslet Parkside ground. There was to be no repeat of Bradford's early season mauling there this time though as Menzies gave them a first half lead when playing with the wind. With several players unavailable through injury, Bradford were not able to prevent a second half equaliser however, and a replay at the same ground was required.

Two more fixtures were played before the replay, a 2-1 friendly success against the Kings Own Scottish Borderers, in which Bradford had to lend their opponents one of their players. As this was played only 24 hours after the Featherstone game then it was no surprise to see the locals devoid of several regulars in their team. A fifth meeting with Leeds then followed, a strike resulting from a *'scrimmage'* in front of goal in the second half seeing Bradford leave the Kirkstall ground with a narrow 1-0 victory. By now they were top of the league, having caught up with their league fixtures, and seeing Hunslet experiencing the 'jitters' as matters came to a climax.

However, the cup final replay came first – and on this occasion there was no doubt who would win straight from the opening exchanges. A goal inside the first two minutes from Menzies set Bradford on their way, Dell adding a second before half time. Menzies added a third after the interval, and despite a spirited fightback from Featherstone, a later Thompson goal saw Bradford victorious by 4 goals to 1 in front of 1500 spectators. The cup was later presented to Bradford captain, Shepherd, by a Miss. Kent, daughter of the president of the Hunslet club, and a gate of over £16 5s was realized. On their return to the town, the Bradford Observer reported that a *'large crowd of football enthusiasts'* met the victorious team at the train station.

The victorious, and yet very different Bradford team to that from the start of the season, was:
Lemoine (goal), **Wells, Smith** (half backs), **N.Thorne, H.Collinson, R.Thorne** *(backs)*, **Matthew, Ingham, Dell, D.Menzies, Thompson** (forwards),

Three days later, attention was turned to the championship decider at home to Hunslet. Played directly after the main rugby match that day, the game attracted *'a large concourse of spectators'*. As was the norm in key games, Bradford took a two-goal lead, the second a Matthews penalty early in the second half, and then conspired to throw away their chances of victory. The strong Leeds based outfit came back strongly in the closing stages to force a draw – and a championship play-off the following Thursday at neutral Kirkstall.

What followed can only be described as *deja-vu*. The 500 or so supporters who travelled to the ground of Leeds FC again saw Bradford race into a two goal lead – Menzies and Thorne on target this time – and again saw them throw it away as Hunslet forced another 2-2 draw! It was originally intended to play extra-time to settle the championship, but with light fading, a tie for the championship was decreed instead – a dramatic end to a dramatic season for Bradford FC!

It was clear that the round ball game had taken off in Bradford. Not only had the reformed association side enjoyed a highly successful season, winning the premier cup competition in the county and sharing a league title, but the public had caught on too. Attendances were such that they were far in excess of those enjoyed by Bradford (Park Avenue) during their final years as a Football League club, and the local press was giving more and more coverage to a game that was rivaling Northern Union (Rugby League) in the area.

The following table has been laid undiscovered in the pages of the local press for many years. Although not all teams completed their fixtures, the table was considered 'final' in an era when many games were left unplayed once the championship had been decided. There was also, at this time, a strict 'cut off' between winter and summer pastimes – the cricket season was about to begin in earnest !

1895/96 WEST YORKSHIRE LEAGUE – FINAL TABLE							
	P	**W**	**D**	**L**	**F**	**A**	**Pts**
Bradford	20	14	3	3	74	31	31
Hunslet	20	15	1	4	75	25	31
Altofts	20	12	4	4	50	32	28
Normanton	20	11	3	6	52	29	25
Leeds	19	11	1	7	45	24	23
Featherstone	18	8	6	4	51	30	22
Pontefract Garrison	19	7	3	9	28	46	17
Halifax	18	7	0	11	40	48	14
Castleford	19	4	2	13	30	57	10
Rothwell	18	3	0	15	10	71	6
Oulton	19	2	2	15	20	71	6
Ferrybridge	withdrawn – record expunged						

OTHER MATCHES.

BRADFORD v. MOSS SIDE (MANCHESTER).

The new Association team of the Bradford Football Club opened its list of home fixtures by playing Moss Side (Manchester). So far as could be gathered, it was the first regular Association fixture ever played at Park Avenue, although a good many years ago an exhibition game was played in this enclosure between Blackburn Rovers and Blackburn Olympic. The gate on Saturday proved very satisfactory to the club officials, who computed that over three thousand persons were present. The match was followed with close interest by the crowd, many persons amongst whom evidently understood the Association rules. On account of it being still holiday season, four reserve men played in the Bradford team, and the Moss Side Club were also somewhat handicapped through the same cause. Moss Side are a well-known amateur combination, and it was confidently expected that the Bradford men would be beaten. As it turned out, however, such was not the case. On the wnole Bradford had the better of the game in both halves. Whyte, Matthews, all the Thornes, and Menzies played exceedingly well, and continually proved themselves superior to their Manchester opponents, while Smith and Shepherd were very safe, and Killick defended smartly. Moss Side had nearly as many corners as Bradford during the first half hour of play, but did nothing with them, and when the home side scored it was from ordinary play. Well on in the first half Smith returned the ball nicely to H. Thorne, who passed it to Whyte, and the latter, who played as well as anyone on the field, kicked a goal. Shortly afterwards, after another long kick by Smith, Matthews with a long shot from near the corner also scored, both Hill and the nearest Manchester back underrunning the ball. Bradford crossed over with a lead of two goals to nothing. Just after the restart, however, Lees sent the ball to McMoraine, who shot it through, and Moss Side thus opened their account. No addition, however, was subsequently made to it, whereas Bradford scored two more goals. Some pretty passing by Whyte, Healey, and Menzies resulted in the last-named, who was close up, being able to shoot through, and later Menzies from a pass by Whyte shot a beautiful goal. Some good work was afterwards shown by Haslam (a very clever player), McMoraine, Clare, and Lee for Moss Side, but at the call of time the home side were left victors by four goals to nil. Something has been already said of the individual merits of the players on both sides, but a word should be added in commendation of the goalkeeping of Hill for the visitors. The teams were as follow:—Bradford: H. Killick, goal; I. Smith and J. Miles, backs; A. Shepherd (captain), R. Thorne, and N. Thorne, half backs; and E. D. Matthews, H. Thorne, Menzies, Whyte, and Healey, forwards. Moss Side (Manchester): Hill, goal; Haslam and Webster, backs; Woodhead, Gulland, and Morris, half backs; and Butt, Smythe, McMoraine, Clare, and Lee, forwards.

BRADFORD FC
1895-96 record

Date	Competition	Opponents	Venue	Result	Score
7/9/1895	Friendly	Swinton (Rotherham)	a	L	0-3
14/9/1895	Friendly	Moss Side (Manchester)	h	W	4-1
21/9/1895	Friendly	Ackworth School	a	W	4-3
24/9/1895	Friendly	Bolton Wanderers	h	L	2-7
28/9/1895	League	Featherstone	h	W	4-2
5/10/1895	League	Hunslet	a	L	1-7
12/10/1895	Friendly	Huddersfield	h	W	4-0
19/10/1895	League	Halifax	h	W	2-0
26/10/1895	LWHC1	Harrogate St.Peters	h	W	8-1
2/11/1895	League	Altofts	a	L	1-3
9/11/1895	League	Oulton	h	W	6-3
16/11/1895	League	Castleford	a	W	2-0
23/11/1895	League	Featherstone	a	D	1-1
30/11/1895	League x	Leeds	h1	W	6-2
7/12/1895	Friendly	Hunslet	h	W	6-0
14/12/1895	League	Normanton	a	W	3-2
21/12/1895	Friendly	Scarborough	h	W	4-0
28/12/1895	LWHC2	Hunslet	h	W	7-4
4/1/1896	League	Halifax	a	L	4-5
11/1/1896?	League	Oulton	a	W	5-1xx
18/1/1896	League	Normanton	h	W	4-0
25/1/1896	Friendly	Pontefract Garrison	h2	W	3-0
1/2/1896	League	Castleford	h	W	2-0
5/2/1896	League	Pontefract Garrison	a	W	6-1
8/2/1896	Friendly	Yorkshire College	h2	W	2-1
15/2/1896	League	Altofts	h	D	2-2
22/2/1896	League	Rothwell	a	W	4-1
29/2/1896	LWHCsf	Leeds	n1	D	2-2
7/3/1896	League	Pontefract Garrison	h	W	9-0
14/3/1896	LWHCsf rep.	Leeds	n2	W	4-0
21/3/1896	League	Leeds	h1	W	2-1
28/3/1896	League	Rothwell	h	W	13-0
4/4/1896	Friendly	Scarborough	a	L	3-6
6/4/1896	LWHC Final	Featherstone	n3	D	1-1
7/4/1896	Friendly	Kings Own Scottish Borderers	h	W	2-1
13/4/1896	League	Leeds	a	W	1-0
22/4/1896	LWHC F. rep	Featherstone	n3	W	4-1
25/4/1896	League	Hunslet	h	D	2-2
30/4/1896	League play off	Hunslet	n4	D	2-2

LWHC = Leeds Workpeople's Hospital Cup
X = match declared void
XX=untraced fixture - score worked out using Bradford's record in Final table
All home games played at Park Avenue except the following: h1=Apperley Bridge, h2=Girlington,
Neutral venues as follows: n1=Hanson Lane, Halifax, n2=Valley Parade, Bradford, n3=Parkside, Hunslet, n4=Kirkstall, Leeds

It is unfortunate that Bradford's run of success could not be continued in the seasons that followed. The West Riding Football Association, formed in the early months of 1896, took over the control of affairs in the immediate vicinity and surprisingly decided against running a league competition for the 1896-97 season. Instead, a knockout cup competition was organised – in which Bradford made it to the semi-final. Following a bye in round one, they went on to defeat Altofts 2-0 and Fryston 5-2, both at home, before bowing out at Huddersfield to Hunslet (1-2). Hunslet went on to defeat Halifax 4-0 in the first West Riding FA cup final at Valley Parade.

Despite victories in many of the friendly fixtures played that season, cup success eluded Bradford FC. They were also defeated in the semi-final of the Leeds Workpeople's Hospital Cup, 0-4 at Headingley to Halifax. Ironically, Hunslet again beat Halifax in the final – 4-1 – in a tie also played at Valley Parade.

What was probably Bradford's only excursion into the prestigious FA Amateur Cup took place in the 1896-97 season. However, old rivals Hunslet put them out in November, following earlier victories over Derby Amateurs and, surprisingly, Sheffield (8-0 & 2-1 respectively).

Bradford was not without league competition for long though, as in 1897 the Sheffield & Hallamshire FA formed a new competition. Thus the first – albeit short lived – Yorkshire League was born. Unfortunately, the locals struggled in their new surroundings in a competition dominated by the South Yorkshire based reserve sides of Football League and Midland League clubs.

The 1897-98 season kicked off with high hopes for the local XI, Harold Collinson elected club captain, and I. Smith vice-captain. They were however reported as being without influential player Jack Eckford, who would later go on to play professionally for Luton Town. Following two friendly fixtures at Park Avenue, the first seeing the return of Bolton Wanderers (who won 3-0) and the second against Accrington FC (who also left Bradford victorious, 3-1). This team was possibly a reincarnation of the original Accrington FC who had been founder members of the Football League in 1888, but after falling on hard times had disbanded around 1896. It was almost certainly not the Accrington Stanley side who came to prominence much later on however.

Bradford's first fixture in the new Yorkshire League was against Sheffield United's second string. Their new campaign could not have got off to a worse start as they were annihilated 10-0 at Bramall Lane. Following a 0-5 reversal at Barnsley St.Peters a first point was then gained at home to Halifax, but it was obvious by then that the Yorkshire League was of a much higher standard than the old West Yorkshire League. Ironically, the West Yorkshire League had been reformed this season, previous rivals such as Altofts and Normanton joining several new sides – Dewsbury, Batley, Wakefield, Harrogate St.Peters among them. Hunslet and Bradford had made a step up in class instead, and both were struggling !

Bradford's first victory of the campaign was a 6-0 success in a friendly at home to Hull Kingston Amateurs in October, although a first league success was to follow soon afterwards when eventual wooden-spoonists Huddersfield were despatched by the same scoreline at park Avenue in November. Unfortunately few people saw the victory, with 10,000 at Valley Parade for the Manningham-Bradford derby in the Northern Union.

Bradford continued to struggle in the league all season, eventually finishing second from bottom in the 10 team league. A 2-1 home defeat of Hunslet was the highlight of a disappointing campaign, their only victory away from home a 1-0 defeat of Huddersfield at Milnsbridge. Attendances were generally lower than they had been in their successful West Yorkshire league season- the 2000 present for the visit of leaders Barnsley in March possibly being the highest. There was to be no success in local cup competitions either – beaten 0-5 in the West Yorkshire Cup semi-final at Dewsbury against Hunslet (this after 5-0 victories over Altofts and Oulton in earlier rounds), and a narrow 2-3 defeat at the new Hunslet ground at Low Road to Leeds in the Leeds Hospital Cup at the same stage of that competition. Hunslet themselves put poor league form aside to again win both cup competitions.

Bradford also entered a reserve side in a new division two (North) of the re-formed West Yorkshire League, playing alongside clubs such as Otley, Menston, Keighley & Bradford Spartans (the latter of whom failed to reappear the following season). This was very much a 'junior' competition compared to division one of the same league, which was titled 'senior division'. A ground at Bankfoot was used by the reserves during the 1897-98 season.

In October 1897, Bradford Spartans (nothing else known about this club except that they had played friendlies the season before) put out this side against Bradford (reserves):

       A.E.Feather (goal), **T.Leathley, G.Duckles** (backs), **D.Chambers, G.E.Helstrip, C.Naylor** (half backs), **W.White, E.Thomas, A.Crossland, A.Clayton, W.H.Fearnside** (forwards)

There was also a Bowling club playing in the same competition alongside Spartans et al. This is likely to have been an experimental 'association' section of the rugby club of the same name and it is possible that they played home fixtures at Greenfield on alternate weekends to the rugby club.

1897/98 –YORKSHIRE LEAGUE – FINAL TABLE

	P	W	D	L	F	A	Pts
Sheffield Utd (res)	18	11	5	2	55	15	27
Mexborough (res)	18	12	2	4	51	22	26
Barnsley St.Peters (res)	18	11	3	4	62	27	25
Doncaster Rov (res)	18	11	2	5	61	26	24
The Wednesday (res)	18	11	1	6	56	26	23
Hunslet	18	7	5	6	32	38	19
Leeds	18	5	1	12	26	52	11
Halifax	18	4	3	11	26	54	11
Bradford	18	3	3	12	26	72	9
Huddersfield	18	2	1	15	14	77	5

West Yorkshire League: Division 2 North ('junior'): winners: Keighley – other sides: Beeston Hill Parish Church (r/u), Renshaw Albion, **Bowling**, Otley, Menston, **Bradford Spartans & Bradford 'A'**. (The latter two teams finished at the foot of the table). Keighley beat Oulton St.Johns (div. 2 South winners) 2-1 in championship match.

Bradford's first team opened the 1898-99 season in new surroundings. The 'Bradford Observer' reported that: *'a vigorous attempt is to be made to infuse renewed life into the Association team...and the result of this experiment will be watched with some interest'.*

The experiment the local press was referring to was that of a relocation of the side to the Bowling Old Lane ground on Birch Lane. Reading between the lines, it is more likely that the 'association' section of the club had actually been 'banished' by the dominant rugby players from Park Avenue. The Birch Lane ground was recognised as being much less accessible than Park Avenue, which now benefited from the opening of the Great Horton tramway, and the local press questioned whether the rugby club's second string would be able to attract gates as high as those attracted by the *'soccer'* players.

The 1898-99 season also saw Bradford reserves in a restructured North division of the West Yorkshire League, which had lost it's senior division (possibly as a result of Northern Union clubs abandoning the Association code as Bradford themselves were about to do!). The ground at Bankfoot was abandoned in favour of the Birch Lane enclosure – and it was here that Leeds United played in October 1898! United won 4-2, but failed to complete their fixtures and failed to reappear the following year. No other reference has ever been made to this first Leeds United side – their history being even more obscure than the very first Bradford City, of which we will find out more over the coming pages.

Bradford's first team made much less progress in cup competition – losing to perennial winners Hunslet in the third round of the West Yorkshire Cup, and at Dewsbury in the Leeds Hospitals Cup (just one week after winning there in the West Yorkshire competition), although a slightly better league campaign was experienced. On this occasion they finished fourth from bottom, and experienced far fewer heavy defeats, but it was clear that all was not well. By the new year, they were back at Park Avenue, with very few games having been played at Birch Lane. The Bowling Old Lane was said to have had an excellent playing surface, so the reason for the part-move back to Park Avenue must have been down to the poor 'gates' experienced at the new ground. Birch Lane was not abandoned completely however, it was obviously still used when their preferred choice was unavailable, and indeed Hunslet were again defeated there in a league fixture in April.

It was also reported that in several games the local side comprised partly of soldiers from the Yorkshire Regiment stationed in Bradford, suggesting that some players had already left the club. There was certainly a problem somewhere, as only 9 men made the journey to Mexborough in April 1899! Furthermore, the club's last game of the season, against champions Wombwell Town (a 0-4 defeat) saw David Menzies keeping goal for the locals! Even the reserves struggled to field a full compliment of players – only 9 making the journey to Keighley in a West Yorkshire League fixture (they still won 2-0 however!)

The writing was certainly on the wall for Bradford FC, the 'association' section was obviously in disarray, and it was no surprise when the club abandoned the round ball game that summer. The side were not really missed however, as the newly formed Bradford Football Association and Bradford & District Football League came into being and commanded the public's attention instead. Former Bradford FC players joined other local clubs instead, notably David Menzies who went to Airedale, and Duncan Menzies, who went to Girlington.

It was an inglorious end to a side who were pioneers of the sport in Bradford, however it was too long before the Park Avenue club abandoned rugby altogether, and in 1907 the professional, and future Football League side came into being there.

The original Bradford side can claim to have been the first club from the city to play in the FA Cup, which they entered in seasons 1897-98 & 1898-99, losing on both occasions at the first stage to South Yorkshire opposition. At Kilnhurst in the first 1st qualifying round they went down 1-3, despite leading at half time when a Matthews shot cannoned off a home defender into the net. *The Bradford side for their first ever FA cup game was:*

Harker (goal), **Smith, Collinson** (backs), **Thorne, Jenkins, Healey** (half backs), **Garner, David Menzies, Matthews, Duncan Menzies, Moore** (forwards)

The following year saw defeat at Parkgate United 4-8, after a 2-2 draw at home, in the 2nd qualifying round. Surprisingly, Bradford FC only entered the FA Amateur Cup once, a popular competition for other local 'senior' sides such as Hunslet.

1898/99 –YORKSHIRE LEAGUE – FINAL TABLE

	P	W	D	L	F	A	Pts
Wombwell Town	18	13	4	1	48	11	30
Doncaster Rov (res)	18	13	1	4	78	20	27
Sheffield Utd (res)	18	12	2	4	55	20	26
The Wednesday (res)	18	12	1	5	58	27	25
Mexborough (res)	18	11	2	5	40	28	24
Hunslet	18	7	3	8	38	27	17
Bradford	18	4	1	13	25	49	9
Sheffield	18	4	1	13	36	65	9
Huddersfield	18	4	1	13	15	73	9
Dewsbury	18	1	2	15	10	78	4

West Yorkshire League North Division (no senior division): Keighley, Ossett, Renshaw Albion, Bowling, Menston, Beeston Hill Parish Church, Otley, Harrogate, Yeadon & **Bradford 'A'. Leeds United withdrew during the season.** Menston & Keighley played in the Bradford & District League the following season.

The old West Yorkshire and Yorkshire Leagues contained some familiar names – although sides such as (the second, and more famous) Leeds United, Huddersfield Town & Halifax Town were still a few years away from being formed !

The sides in the early county leagues were in some cases (such as Bradford) 'association' sections of the established Northern Union (Rugby League) sides, or sides allowed to use the grounds of their rugby counterparts, as 'soccer' was seen as a potentially profit making means. Halifax were formed in September 1894 following a meeting at the Black Swan Hotel, and at first using a field at the end of Pickles Lane (now known as Gibraltar Road). After just one season there, a move was made to the Pheasant Ground at Pellon. The club merged with the town's rugby club in 1895 and at first played on the cricket ground at Hanson Lane, Thrum Hall. They later used the main pitch when the rugby team were away from home. The Pheasant Ground, and another at Newstead were still occasionally used however. Unfortunately the 'association' section floundered as it came under increasing opposition from the better established rugby section.

Huddersfield FC were formed in 1895 as an offshoot of the Huddersfield Cricket & Athletic club, who were based at Fartown. However, when Bradford played at Huddersfield in the 1897-98 season they played the home side on a ground at Milnsbridge, and the following year at the town's Technical College, suggesting that Fartown was not available to the soccer team all the time, if ever.

The Leeds club, formed on 22nd February 1894 first played at Harehills Road, Roundhay, and also used grounds at Headingley (until ousted by the Rugby club) and Meanwood (The previously mentioned Kirkstall ground probably being one at Headingley). They disbanded after losing 0-8 to Hunslet at the end of the 1897-98 campaign, however, with their playing fortunes and finances floundering. The Yorkshire League itself, like Bradford FC's soccer section, appears to have become defunct at the end of the 1898-99 season.

Park Avenue – 1893. *Unfortunately a decent OS map of the area at the time of Bradford FC's successful 1895-96 campaign is unavailable – so this poor quality image will have to do instead ! The 'pavilion' on the map is no doubt part of the half-length stand along the cricket side of the rugby field. Horton Park Station served Park Avenue well over the years, while Canterbury Avenue now covers Horton Villa.*

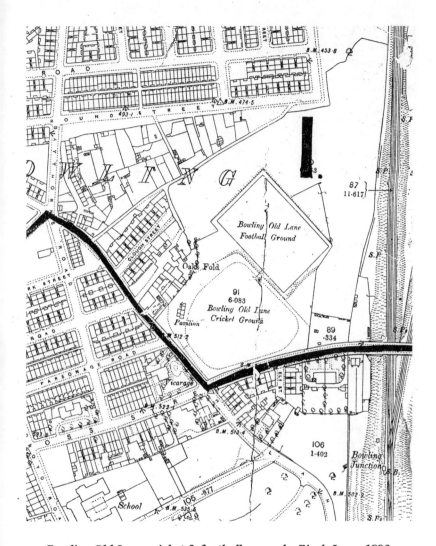

Bowling Old Lane cricket & football grounds, Birch Lane, 1893.
*Bradford FC played some games at the latter, which was already a well
established rugby ground, during the 1898-99 season. Bradford Northern –
formed when Bradford FC finally abandoned the rugby code in 1907 - briefly
used the same ground some years later. Although the cricket ground still
exists, the former football ground is now covered by housing and the school
on Ryan Street.*

Public Notices.

FOOTBALL.—BRADFORD ASSOCIATION.

BOLTON WANDERERS
(FULL LEAGUE TEAM, WITH RESERVES) v
BRADFORD DISTRICT,
AT VALLEY PARADE, on MONDAY, Sept. 2nd. Kick off 5.45 p.m.
Admission, 6d and 3d ; Boys, 1d.

CITY OF BRADFORD.
TURKISH BATHS FOR LADIES

Notice is hereby given that, COMMENCING on MONDAY, September 9th, and on EVERY MONDAY until further notice, the TURKISH BATHS at the Corporation Baths, Thornton Road, will be RESERVED EXCLUSIVELY FOR LADIES, from Nine a.m. to Eight p.m. during the period from October 1st to March 31st, and from Nine a.m. to Nine p.m. from April 1st to September 30th.

Admission will be obtained by the ordinary entrance to the Women's Baths.

The charge will be ONE SHILLING each Person, this including either a Turkish or Vapour Bath, with the usual Warm or Cold Showers.

Lady Masseuses will be in attendance, and Lady Patrons may depend on receiving every civility and attention.

By Order,
FREDERICK STEVENS, Town Clerk.
Town Hall, Bradford, 30th August, 1901.

ARMITAGE, PAWNBROKER,
60, ROSSE STREET, BROWNROYD, Bradford.

DRESS SKIRTS—A SPECIALITY.
ALL SIZES STOCKED.
FIT GUARANTEED.
ANY STYLE MADE TO ORDER AT A DAYS NOTICE.
LUTHER HILL,
MARKET HALL.

An advertisement from the 'Bradford Daily Argus' (31/8/1901) for Bolton Wanderers' visit to Valley Parade. This was certainly not their first visit to Bradford, having played at Park Avenue at least twice previously.

3
THE FIRST BRADFORD CITY

BRADFORD & DISTRICT LEAGUE 1901-02

The Bradford & District Football League was formed in September 1899, seven months after the formation of the local Football Association. Amongst the dominant sides in it's first season were Rawdon, Airedale (a side based at Undercliffe) and Girlington, who played home games at Manningham Rugby Club's Valley Parade ground in order to accommodate the large crowds who attended their home games.

Prior to the formation of the local league, the few local sides playing competitive fixtures – Bradford FC, Bowling and Bradford Spartans in particular - had plied their trade in the various short lived county leagues. Unfortunately by the time of the formation of the local league, not one of these three sides existed as a soccer team, a pity considering their role as pioneers of the sport in Bradford.

The Bradford & District League, which had no trouble attracting sides of a suitable quality in it's early years of existence, actually gained several sides when the West Yorkshire League was surprisingly discontinued for the 1901-02 season. One team elected straight into the first division this season were newcomers **BRADFORD CITY.** Of some significance, Bradford had received its 'charter' in 1897, allowing the town to rename itself a city. It was surely only a matter of time therefore, that a side from 'worstedopolis' should adopt the title 'Bradford City FC'. As we shall see, this side was to be a welcome addition to a league trying to establish itself as one of the strongest in the county, with the standard of play having improved each season since it's formation yet which was still considered inferior to the nearby Heavy Woollen League. The Heavy Woollen competition by this time boasted a 'Senior League' of 12 teams as well as two 'Junior leagues'

Why a team who had apparently just been formed were elected into the top division of the Bradford & District League (of which there were four divisions in all), alongside its established sides has not been possible to ascertain, but it is ironic that the professional Bradford City were elected straight into the Football League upon their formation in 1903! There is no record of an amateur Bradford City FC even playing friendly fixtures the previous season, so we can only assume that it was indeed a completely new club.

It seems that the rise of the new City club, who were to be based at the Greenfield sports ground at Dudley Hill, was actually formed at the expense of one Harewood Recreation FC. Harewood, who played home games at Boldshay Fields, were founder members of the Bradford & District League in the 1899-1900 season, occupying a mid-table position in the first division that year. The following season they, along with Airedale FC pushed champions Girlington all the way in the race for the title. In their side were at least three players who appeared in the Bradford City side the following year - notably Bebbington, Butler & Boydell. Months later, as City took their place in the Bradford league's top division for the 1901-02 season, Harewood appeared in division three ! One can only surmise that their two division demotion was entirely voluntary having lost several key players, or that the side had reformed after becoming defunct during the summer of 1902. Their Boldshay Fields ground was actually close to, or identical to, that used by Church Hill FC who were promoted to the district league's first division the same season as Bradford City joined the competition.

There was also a Greenfield FC around in the two seasons preceding Bradford City's formation – it is likely that they used the same Greenfield ground as City, but are unlikely to have been linked to the club, playing in division 2B of the Bradford & District league for the 1899-1900 season, and in division three the following year. This club were more likely to have been linked to the successful Greenfield Northern Union (Rugby League) club of that era.

The first reference to the new Bradford City came when Bolton Wanderers returned to the city to play a Bradford & District representative side at Valley Parade on Monday September 2nd 1901, kicking off at 5.45pm. It was clear that the Wanderers had once again returned as 'missionaries' for the match, against what was considered the 'elite' of the Bradford & District League. However, in front of a rather disappointing attendance of only 600, who paid 6d or 3d for the privilege (with an extra 6d to sit in the main stand) *'the game did not prove very exciting'* according to the 'Bradford Observer'. Relevant to this book, however, is the fact that among the names in the local line up were Mssrs. Bebbington & Butler from the previously unheard of Bradford City club.

The teams for this game were:
   Bolton Wanderers: Sutcliffe (goal), Brown, Woodfall (backs), Fatchett, Freebairn, Burnison (half backs), Nicol, Picken, McKee, Barlow, Tracey (forwards),
Bradford & District select: Wortley *(Clayton)* (goal), **Bebbington** *(Bradford City),* Ellison *(Rawdon)* (backs), Needham *(Cullingworth),* Gilroy

(Airedale), David Menzies *(Airedale)* (half backs), Moore *(Rawdon),* Whettal *(Clayton),* **Butler** *(Bradford City),* Hargreaves *(Menston),* Duncan Menzies *(Girlington)* (forwards)

Presumably, trials were held for the local XI, the two players from the fledgling Bradford City FC being selected alongside those from better-known sides of the time. Both Bebbington and Butler were no doubt well known to the team selectors already, having turned out for Harewood Recreation the previous season. Of the two, Butler was described as having a good chance to score early on in the game, before Wanderers took the lead for the first time. Before half time, Hargreaves had equalised for the locals, but the professional outfit took control in the second period, running out 3-1 winners, with goals from Burnison, McKee & Picken. Just twelve days later, Bradford City played their first ever league fixture at Cullingworth.....

Despite some pre-season withdrawals from the league, nine clubs commenced the season in the first division of the Bradford & District League for the 1901-02 season - champions Girlington, District Cup holders Rawdon, plus Airedale, Clayton, Cullingworth, Otley, Belgrave, Church Hill, who were promoted at the last minute, and newcomers Bradford City.

The all-new Bradford City FC played their first competitive fixture at Cullingworth on Saturday September 14th 1901. Where exactly Cullingworth's football field was at this time is unclear, although it could well have been that at Royd Wood, which the village club was certainly using in the 1920's. A Mr.Albert Sugden was said to have kicked off, with City taking the upper hand after a fairly even opening and eventually triumphing with a goal in each half. Who these first goalscorers were was never actually reported in the local press, and as a result those responsible for the first goals ever scored by a Bradford City side will never be known !

The team for City's first ever competitive fixture was:
Parsons (goal), **Bebbington, Anker** (backs), **Donald, Booth, Firth** (half backs), **Hall, Butler, Sowerby, Norman, Boydell** (forwards),

City were due to play their first ever home game, at Greenfield, a week later against Belgrave FC. For whatever reason the fixture was not played, due possibly to the unavailability of the ground, which was likely to have been shared with other clubs such as Greenfield Northern Union club of the Bradford Junior Rugby League, or due to internal problems which Belgrave seemed to have been experiencing that season (more on that later).

The club's next fixture was fulfilled however, away at Church Hill FC's Harewood Street ground, where it was reported that A.Davies of City was turning out against his former club. The game resulted in a second victory for Bradford City as they raced into a three-goal lead thanks to strikes from Boydell (2) and Sowerby. Despite a strong come-back from the Church Hill side, when they scored twice, a fourth, un-named goalscorer, tied things up for the victors. It was reported in the local press that Bowden and Church Hill's Dolan had been sent from the field for fighting, the City player later suspended for two weeks by the Bradford Football Association (Dolan failed to appear before the FA panel and was subsequently suspended until he saw fit to do so).

One week later Bradford City used Greenfield for the first time, albeit in treacherous conditions when they entertained former West Yorkshire League outfit Otley FC. Butler's opening goal for City was cancelled out by Otley's Wilkinson before half time, but the second period saw the visitors routed as Boydell (2), Davies, Norman and Firth saw the homesters cruise to a 6-1 victory. City by now led the league, ahead of Airedale FC and Belgrave FC, the latter of whom had won their two opening games.

The first points were dropped by Bradford City in a goal-less draw at Rawdon on October 12th, although City maintained a two-point lead over Airedale, who had a game in hand (Greenfield were also top of the Bradford Junior Rugby League at the time).

There was no game the following week, but on October 26th City met Airedale FC at the ground of the latter. In front of what was described in the local press as a 'large' attendance, it was the home team who proved victorious in an exciting game. Dennison, the Airedale centre beat Parsons in the City goal for the game's opening goal, before a brace from Boocock made the score 3-0. Butler pulled goal back for City before half time, and soon after the interval Sowerby reduced arrears further. However, Dennison completed his hat-trick with two more strikes before what the local broadsheets described as 'a lucky point' for City, making the score 5-3 in Airedale's favour. Themselves now at head of the league table, Airedale had been one of the leading lights on the local 'association' scene since their formation in the late 1890's, during which time they had started out playing on a ground on Moorside Road, Fagley before making the short journey to Undercliffe.

Clayton FC were the second visitors to Greenfield early in November, and like Otley before them, they were convincingly dispatched as City got back to winning ways. It was Clayton who actually went in front through a goal from Bowden, only for Davies to equalize only a moment later. Boydell and then Booth made the score 3-1 before Bowden scored his second for Clayton before half time. Boydell scored what seems to have been Bradford City's first hat-trick with two further goals in the second half to put City back on top of the league with a 5-2 victory. With 2 points for a victory, their record so far was P6, W4, D1, L1, goals for 20, goals against 10, points 9.

Things looked even sweeter for the league newcomers when, one week later, Airedale went down to improving Church Hill as City demolished Belgrave FC 5-0 away from home. Although the match was not reported on in the press, City could be seen to be four points clear of Airedale, who had played two games less.

Following this, Girlington FC then left Greenfield with a narrow 3-2 defeat, the Bradford City side being basically the same as that which started the campaign at Cullingworth, but with Davies having replaced Sowerby in attack. It is also known that Firth would keep goal if Parsons was unavailable, and that Buswell was another name in the side on occasions.

City were then surprisingly beaten at Otley in what was described as a 'very well contested' game. The 'Bradford Daily Argus' commented that:
'Hull played a good game for Bradford City, but he was a little too fond of tricks and on one occasion he was cautioned for kicking.'

Cullingworth were then defeated 3-1, although they put up a tremendous fight when you consider that the village side played the game with only nine men. In later years, the Cullingworth side would turn their attentions to the Keighley & District soccer. One of the longest lasting of the Bradford & District League sides of 1901-02, by the early 1920's they had lifted all three of Keighley's top soccer competitions – namely the Keighley & District League, F.A. Cup & Charity Cup competitions.

On December 7th 1901 Bradford City travelled *away from home* to the ground of Girlington FC – Valley Parade ! It is amazing to think that a Bradford City side could have played an away fixture at the ground over 18 months before a side of that name would make it their own. Despite another narrow 3-2 victory for City in this match, 'Sportsman' of the 'Bradford Daily Telegraph' was moved to write;
'neither side seem to have shown good football. In the forwards there was too much playing to the wing men, the three inside passing game being neglected altogether.' He continued, *' Before the locals can expect to make the game attractive they must cultivate the short passing game which is most effective.'*

It seems that away trip to the ground made famous by the current Bradford City was the last league game played by the old City side during 1901. A fixture at Clayton four days before Christmas was cancelled 'on account of the frost', as was another at home to Rawdon. One game was played however, an 'ordinary' (friendly) match at home to Pudsey, which was won by a single goal to nil - the return early in the new year saw Pudsey gain revenge with another narrow victory, this time by 3 goals to 2.

Another match was cancelled on January 10th 1902. In this case, it was City's first ever Bradford & District Cup tie, against a side they had already cancelled a home league fixture with, Belgrave FC. The reason for this cancellation can be much more easily explained, as it was reported only days later in the 'Bradford Daily Telegraph' that the Belgrave team had disbanded and withdrawn from league competition.

After a break of over a month, Bradford City finally played another competitive fixture – a 3-1 victory in the District Cup against second division Swaine Hill United, although there is no trace of a match report, or of the City goalscorers available. However, a much bigger cup fixture was on the horizon for the locals. Their next opponents were crack Leeds outfit Hunslet FC in the West Yorkshire Cup, possibly returning to the city for the first time since their epic battles with Bradford FC in the 1890's. Hunslet were established FA Amateur Cup entrants, having entertained the mighty Bishop Auckland FC in the previous year's competition, and it was no surprise then that City were defeated 1-4 (reported as being 1-3 in some newspapers of the time) at Greenfield. Despite being considered the top team in the West Riding, Hunslet were surprisingly knocked out of the competition by top Heavy Woollen League side Mirfield United in the very next round. (The Mirfield side went out in the semi-final to a strong Altofts outfit) In future years, Hunslet would lose their ground and go into 'hibernation', and although they never actually officially reformed, members of the Hunslet committee were instrumental in forming Leeds City FC – forerunners of the current Leeds United.

The Hunslet team, the most redoubtable of all those played that season by City was: **Wortley** (goal), **Hooper, Kirkwood** (backs), **Heffron, Moon, Tennant** (half backs), **Duncanson, Keech, Little, Tierney & Egginton** (forwards).

The following week, Bradford City's return match with Airedale was cancelled due to snow, on a day when the only Bradford & District League fixture played was at Valley Parade, Girlington thrashing Clayton 12-0 to move closer to the leading two.

A fortnight later, City played a third round tie in the District Cup, defeating another division two side Birkenshaw St.Pauls, according to the local 'Daily Argus' 7-0 – a match which seems to indicates the side's record victory in their short existence – although this was been reported as being only 6-0 in the

'Bradford Observer' & 'Yorkshire Daily Observer'. Two more emphatic league victories followed for City, 4-0 in the re-arranged fixture at Clayton, and then 5-0 against Church Hill, proving that the Hunslet defeat had not affected their league form.

At this point of the season, and with the Church Hill score included, the Bradford & District League's first division table looked like this: (courtesy of the 'Bradford Daily Argus')

	P	W	L	D	F	A	Pts
Bradford City	12	9	2	1	39	18	19
Airedale	8	6	1	1	35	11	13
Girlington	9	5	2	2	40	9	12
Otley	8	4	3	1	18	18	9
Church Hill	9	4	5	0	12	27	8
Clayton	11	3	7	1	19	49	7
Cullingworth	10	2	7	1	16	30	5
Rawdon	10	1	6	3	12	24	5
Belgrave	10	2	7	1	12	43	5

Unfortunately the table above is somewhat inaccurate as win & losses don't seem to add up, neither do goals for & against. City's 5-0 success against Belgrave doesn't seem to be taken account of, despite Belgrave's record still being included. It looks as if all of Belgrave's results have been deleted from the records of their opponents, although the table does not add up even then ! There again, newspapers were full of league tables from a number of sports that did not 'add-up' at this time.

Two epic Bradford & District Cup-ties against Girlington at the neutral Park Avenue ground then took priority for Bradford City.

Girlington had been defeated in the previous season's final and desperately wanted to make it third time lucky, however, they had been defeated twice in the league by newcomers City and a big crowd anticipated a close game.

The best report of the tie comes from Ronnie Wharton in his book 'The Best of Bradford Amateur Football'....

'City's right wing pairing of Butler and Hull proved a constant threat, causing all sorts of problems for Hubbert and young Knowles in Girlington's defence. Keeper Gott came to the rescue on several occasions, but had no chance when City's giant centre forward Norman scored from close range. The one goal divided the teams at the interval, but only two minutes into the

(second) half, City went 2-0 up when a fine run by Boydell was turned into the net by Butler. Girlington's right wing Gilroy started to make strides down the flank and it was from a shot by the winger which City keeper Parsons could only parry, that Menzies opened Girlington's account. City should have gone 3-1 up when Boydell failed to score with an open goal facing. Girlington came back with an equaliser when Menzies put away his second goal after Butt had done the spadework.'

The replay a few days later was played at the same venue, strong winds marring the game, which was won by a single goal from Girlington forward Denby, who latched onto a poor clearance from Parsons, this despite Butler being the best forward on the field. It was Girlington's first victory over City in four attempts, and it put them into the district final where at last they overcame Airedale 2-1. Included in the Girlington side was Duncan Menzies, a player who had previously turned out for Bradford FC in the Yorkshire League from 1897. A sign of the growing importance of the round ball game in the city was the fact that posters were placed around Bradford advertising the local cup semi-finals. This was already common practice for Bradford and Manningham rugby fixtures, and many posters by now displayed both rugby and 'soccer' fixtures together.

While City and Girlington had been engaging themselves in their semi final ties, Airedale had meanwhile put themselves in contention for the Bradford League championship with a thumping 11-0 defeat of struggling Clayton. Despite City then defeating Rawdon to the tune of 5-1 at Greenfield, it was the Undercliffe based side who held the upper hand by now, and the teams still had to meet in what would be a title decider.

The championship decider was played at Greenfield on 26th April. Although the local press were by now eagerly anticipating the forthcoming cricket season, and as a result were reducing their coverage of local soccer (and that included ignoring final league tables!), there was just enough written to be able to determine what happened in this crucial decider.

In what was described as a *'stubborn fight'*, in front of a fair sized crowd, the first half remained goal-less. However, Davies gave City the lead just after the break, and for a while it looked as if Bradford City would win the Bradford & District League title at their first attempt. Unfortunately, though, a late equaliser for Airedale meant that it was they who lifted the 'Yorkshire Sports Shield' instead, a championship triumph that was described as much due to 'good management as to the play' at a later Bradford FA presentation evening. Ironically, David Menzies, another ex-Bradford FC player was in the Airedale side that season !

Although it was not known at the time, the 1-1 draw with Airedale was to be the final match ever played by the original Bradford City. In their only season they had come close to collecting two sets of silverware, denied by Girlington in the District Cup, and by Airedale in the league. Yet still we know very little else about this first Bradford City club. There are no mentions of the team's colours or where the club's headquarters were based, neither are there details of the club officials and to the background of the side. The only information we can glean about those players who turned out for the club are from match reports in local newspapers of the time.

What is known is that when the 1902-03 season commenced there was no Bradford City in any league competition. Neither was there a Girlington, who had intended joining a revived West Yorkshire League that season alongside Airedale and Rawdon. (Girlington did reform, briefly, a few years later) Airedale actually fielded a side in both the West Yorkshire and Bradford & District Leagues during 1902-03. During the summer, officials of the West Yorkshire League had actually contacted the Bradford City club with regard to them joining the competition...how things may have been different had they done so !

It is likely that most of Bradford City players joined the myriad of new clubs that appeared in newly founded leagues around Bradford over the next season or so. None of them appeared in any of the newly formed professional Bradford City line-ups in their inaugural 1903-04 campaign, that side having to 'import' players from elsewhere due to a dearth of locals considered to be of Football League standard. Of those I have been able to trace, A.Davies seems to have rejoined Church Hill for the 1902-03 season, while Bebbington joined Airedale's West Yorkshire League side. Also playing the same league that season were Anker, Hull & Butler, all in the colours of Rawdon, who struggled at the foot of the table. By now, all that remained of the original Bradford City FC was Greenfield, and it is likely that we shall never know why this club disbanded after one relatively successful season.

BRADFORD & DISTRICT CUP 1901-02
(winners shown first)

1st round
Airedale...6   Park View...1
Manningham St.Pauls...2   West Park...0
Rawdon...4   Shipley...3
Swaine Hill United...4   Eccleshill...0 (after 2-2 draw)
Bradford City w/o   v   Belgrave
Byes: Great Horton, Oakenshaw, Sedgefield Rovers, Menston, Cullingworth, Otley, Church Hill, Birkenshaw St.Pauls, Clayton, St.Judes, Girlington,

2nd round
Airedale...4   Otley...0
Bradford City...3   Swaine Hill United...1
Church Hill...3   Menston...2
Clayton...3   Oakenshaw...0
Cullingworth...4   Sedgefield Rovers...3
Girlington...3   St.Judes...1
Great Horton...4   Birkenshaw St. Pauls...2
     (Birkenshaw through following protest)
Manningham St.Pauls...2   Rawdon...0

3rd round
Airedale...5   Church Hill...1
Bradford City...6   Birkenshaw St.Pauls...1
Cullingworth...3   Manningham St.Pauls...0
Girlington...6   Clayton...1

Semi-finals
Airedale...4   Cullingworth...3   (at Valley Parade)
Girlington...1 **Bradford City...0**   (after 2-2 draw) (both at Park Avenue)

Final
Girlington...2   Airedale...1 (at Park Avenue)

BRADFORD CITY
1901-02 record

Date	Competition	Opponents	Venue	Result	Score
14/9/1901	League	Cullingworth	a	W	2-0
21/9/1901	League	Belgrave	h	not played	
28/9/1901	League	Church Hill	a	W	4-2
5/10/1901	League	Otley	h	W	6-1
12/10/1901	League	Rawdon	a	D	0-0
26/10/1901	League	Airedale	a	L	3-5
2/11/1901	League	Clayton	h	W	5-2
9/11/1901	League	Belgrave	a	W	5-0
16/11/1901	League	Girlington	h	W	3-2
23/11/1901	League	Otley	a	L	1-3
30/11/1901	League	Cullingworth	h	W	3-1
7/12/1901	League	Girlington	a	W	3-2
14/12/1901	Friendly	Pudsey	h	W	1-0
21/12/1901	League	Clayton	a	not played	
28/12/1901	League	Rawdon	h	not played	
11/01/1902	Bfd. Dist. Cup 1	Belgrave	h	not played	
18/01/1902	Friendly	Pudsey	a	L	2-3
25/01/1902	Bfd. Dist. Cup 2	Swaine Hill Utd	h	W	3-1
1/2/1902	West Yorks. Cup	Hunslet	h	L	1-4
8/2/1902	League	Airedale	h	not played	
22/2/1902	Bfd. Dist. Cup 3	Birkenshaw St.Pauls	h	W	6-0
8/3/1902	League	Clayton	a	W	4-0
15/3/1902	League	Church Hill	h	W	5-0
22/3/1902	Bfd.Dist. Cup SF	Girlington	Pk Ave	D	2-2
29/3/1902	Bfd.Dist.Cup SF r	Girlington	Pk Ave	L	0-1
12/4/1902	League	Rawdon	h	W	5-1
26/4/1902	League	Airedale	h	D	1-1

Possibly the only surviving photograph to contain details of the original Bradford City FC. Their District Cup semi-final tie against Girlington is advertised on the outside wall of the 'Jolly Butchers' in Rawson Place. The other tie – between Airedale and Cullingworth - is also advertised, along with Bradford's Northern Union fixture at home to Salford.

THE ASSOCIATION GAME.

BRADFORD AND DISTRICT CUP.

THIRD ROUND.

Church Hill v. Airedale.—This tie was played on the Church Hill ground in the presence of a very good gate. The enclosure was in a shocking condition, and outside the rope matters were even worse. The rivalry between the clubs is of the keenest, and when the Hill men secured an advantage in the opening moves their supporters were exultant as to the result. The going was heavy, and perhaps it was due to this fact that Airedale escaped at this point, the home team's work on the left and centre being quite value for a goal. The visitors, however, at last got on the move, and Welsh passing well out to the left, Boocock got in a centre after beating the back. This Jones fastened upon, and banged into the net. Just after this Church Hill ought to have drawn level, Jackson failing to gather the ball from a centre from the left, but the Hill forwards were slow, and Bouchier got up in time to avert disaster at the expense of a corner. The home side claimed a goal hereabouts, but found the referee against them, and at the interval the score was—Airedale, one goal; Church Hill, none. Immediately on resuming the visitors increased their lead, Lupton accepting a neat pass from Boocock, and shooting past Millhouse. This was followed by a fine goal for the home side, who, however, were soon once more two goals down as a consequence of a penalty given against them, and which was taken charge of by the popular "Banty." Jones scored again for Airedale, and Brown put on another point before the finish, Airedale going into the semi-finals with a victory of five goals to one goal.

Girlington v. Clayton.—In view of the result of the recent League game between these teams, this tie at Valley Parade was looked upon as a foregone conclusion, and the popular view was borne out in a six goals to one victory for Girlington. Right away the home side began scoring, J. Hargreave finding the net with a screw shot. Then the Clayton left (Bowden and Naylor) got off, but were not well supported, and play was soon at the other end, where Denby put on a second goal. For some time after this the game was more even, and Naylor and Bowden were continually troubling Girlington's defence. There was a lack of finish, however, in the villagers' work. At last Naylor got through, and he was not slow in making good use of the opportunity. For a time the home team had rather the worse of the argument, but Menzies set Hargreave off on the left, and the winger's parting shot found the net, Girlington turning round with a three to one lead. On resuming, Gilroy tested Smith, the Clayton goalie, with a good shot, and the latter clearing, play veered again, both Denby and Farley having to retire as a result of injuries. Girlington got on top again, however, and Hargreave put on another goal, and the tie was safe for the home team, who eventually won with great ease.

Bradford City v. Birkenshaw St. Paul's.—On the City's ground at Greenfield. The St. Paul's team were no match for their more experienced opponents, who won the tie by six goals to none. The game was marred by a serious accident to Dobson, the St. Paul's goalkeeper, who, as the result of a collision with one of the City forwards, had to be carried from the field, his injury being a broken leg. He was removed to the Royal Infirmary, and late last night he was reported to be progressing favourably.

Cullingworth v. Manningham St. Paul's.—At Cullingworth, before a good attendance. The visitors on occasion showed some good form, but generally were over-played by their opponents, who won by three goals to none.

DRAW FOR THE SEMI-FINALS.

Girlington v. Bradford City.
Airedale v. Cullingworth.

Attercliffe v. Hunslet.—At Attercliffe, where the

WEST YORKSHIRE CUP.—First Round.

Airedale v. Fryston.—This tie was played on the former club's ground at Undercliffe. Airedale won the toss, and chose to play down hill, but with the sun in their eyes, and a strong breeze which blew diagonally across the ground was of little assistance to them. Just at the commencement the home team had slightly the better of the argument, but Fryston displayed some good combination on the left and centre, and some very steady work by A. Stone and Parkinson at back was too much for the opposing forwards, who were being constantly beaten by the pace at which the ball travelled. Ultimately the Fryston right wing secured possession, and the forward line, beating up skilfully against the wind, secured a corner, from which Ward scored. Midfield play succeeded, and then Boocock headed strongly into the visitors' goal. Shaw sent the ball back to the left-winger, who promptly placed it in the net. Thus at the interval the sides were level. On resuming, Fryston at once developed a strong attack, during which Bouchier brought down an opponent foully, and a goal to the visitors followed from the penalty kick. The siege on the Airedale goal continued for some time longer, but at length David Menzies placed Welsh in possession, and the development of the movement found Boocock, Dennison, and the ex-Rawdon man in front of the Fryston goal. Here Dennison was coolly held by a visiting back, and the penalty being entrusted to Boocock, the youngster safely registered a goal. Again the scores were level, and though Fryston continued to have the better of the argument, they could not get through, and the game ended in a draw—two goals each.

Bradford City v. Hunslet.—There was a fair number of spectators of this tie on the City's ground at Greenfield. The ground was soft, and the players found a footing difficult. In the first movements of the game Butler missed a fine opportunity from a cross by Boydell, but latterly the left-winger beat Hooper, and rattled the ball into the net. After this Hunslet gave Parsons and his backs some work, but the City were very often dangerous, and with a shade of luck should have scored again. Then a change came over the game. Keogh, obtaining a centre by Eggington, put on the equalising goal, and soon afterwards Tierney, the inside left, again beat Parsons, Hunslet thus leading by two to one at half-time, after having had the worse of the play. On resuming the City were early aggressive, but Hunslet once again got the upper hand, and Tierney put through from a scramble. A fourth goal followed off one of the home backs, and Hunslet had now the game well in hand. Though the City tried hard to the finish, they could not break down the visitors' defence, the Leeds men winning by four goals to one.

Girlington v. Savile Town Clarence. Welling

ASSOCIATION.

INTER-LEAGUE MATCH.

	Goals.		Goals.
English League	6	Scottish League	3

THE LEAGUE.—Division 1.

Sunderland	2	Stoke	0
Wolverhampton Wan.	3	Liverpool	1
Bolton Wanderers	2	Aston Villa	2
Derby County	1	Bury	0
Grimsby Town	1	Everton	0
Manchester City	2	Newcastle United	0
Nottingham Forest	2	Sheffield Wednesday	0
Notts County	4	Sheffield United	0
Small Heath	2	Blackburn Rovers	0

Division 2.

Burnley	6	Gainsborough Trinity	0
Bristol City	1	Leicester Fosse	0
Barnsley	2	Blackpool	0
Burslem Port Vale	4	Chesterfield	2
Doncaster Rovers	2	Burton United	0
Lincoln City	1	Glossop	0
Middlesbrough	3	Preston North End	0
West Bromwich Albion	4	Newton Heath	0
Woolwich Arsenal	3	Stockport County	0

WEST YORKSHIRE CUP.—Third Round.
Replayed Ties.

Altofts	1	Huddersfield	0
Beeston Hill Parish Ch.	2	Airedale	1
Oulton	3	Southowram St. Anne's	0

BRADFORD AND DISTRICT LEAGUE.
First Division.

Bradford City	4	Clayton	0
Girlington	2	Rawdon	0

Second Division.

Manston Reserve	3	Birkenshaw St. Paul's	1
Sedgefield Rangers	3	Park View	0

Third Division.

Harewood Recreation	1	Manningham St. Mark's	1
Manningham St. Paul's	1	Shipley	1

Fourth Division.

Bradford Rovers	2	Bramley Street Mission	2

LEEDS AND DISTRICT LEAGUE.

Beckett Clarence	1	Morley Reserve	0
Central	3	Holbeck Moorville	0
Fryston	1	Woodlesford	0
Harehills	4	Leeds Northern	0
Normanton Parish Ch.	3	Rothwell W. Rose Res.	0

NICHOLSON CUP.—Third Round.
Replayed Tie.

Leeds Speedwell	1	Hunslet St. Joseph's	0

STOKER CUP.—First Round.

Garforth	4	Tadcaster	0
Garforth Parish Church	1	Aberford	1
Wetherby	2	Church Fenton	0

HEAVY WOOLLEN DISTRICT LEAGUE.

Batley	4	Saville Town Clarence	1
Dewsbury St. Matthew's	0	Dewsbury and Saville	0
Dewsbury Caltic	3	Heckmondwike Swifts	1
Hartshead	2	Boothroyd White Star	1
Mirfield United	1	Ravensthorpe Clarence	1
Ossett Juniors	2	Morley	1

WHEATLEY CUP.

Shepley Bridge	9	Heckmondwike Parish Ch.	1

HALIFAX AND DISTRICT LEAGUE.

Sowerby Bridge	3	St. Augustine's	1

HUDDERSFIELD AND DISTRICT CUP.—First Round.
Replayed Tie.

Crosland Moor	3	West End	0

BRADFORD AND DISTRICT MEDAL COMPETITION.
Third Round.

Bradford Pin Co.	3	Rawdon Reserve	0
St. Cuthbert's	2	Girlington Shamrock	0

Replayed Tie.

Brownroyd	1	West Bowling	0

BRADFORD SCHOOLS CUP.—Second Round.

Belle Vue	3	Lorne Street	0
Drummond Road	1	Horton Bank Top	0
Hanson	3	Lilycroft	2
Whetley Lane	1	Parish Church	1

OTHER MATCHES.

Chickenley	5	Moorlands	3
Darlington	8	Stockton St. John's	0
Dewsbury Ebenezer	2	Westborough	1
Dewsbury Unitarians	4	Earlsheaton	2
Dewsbury White Star	4	Batley Carr	1
Elland Ramsden's O.B.	2	Wyke Parish Church	0
Farnley Ironworks	2	Royal Artillery (Leeds)	0
Halifax Boys' Brigade	4	Bradford Boys' Brigade	0
Harrogate St. Luke's	2	Harrogate Harlow	2
Hunslet	6	Rothwell White Rose	0
Leeds Parish Church	2	Leeds All Souls'	4
Methley Rovers	5	Purston United	0
Oakenshaw	5	Wyke	1
Scarborough Pensholme	8	West End Harriers	1
Scarborough Raleigh	2	Queen's United	2
Scarborough Utopians	7	Pickering	1
Staleybridge Rovers	2	Barrow	0
Thornaby	1	Willington Athletic	0

Bradford and District.

Croft & Perkins	2	Chelmsford United	1
Eccleshill	4	Pudsey	3
Great Horton	4	Cullingworth Reserve	3
Greengates St. John's	2	Westfield Crescent	1
Lister Hills	3	Yalley United Reserve	3
Norlands	2	Villa Rangers	2
St. John's	1	St. Mary's	1
Whetley United	2	Marshfield	0

Long lost leagues & teams – results from the Yorkshire Daily Observer,
Monday March 10th 1902

4
'ORDINARY MATCHES'
1902-03

At first glance it seemed that the name of Bradford City was missing from the fixtures when the 1902-03 season commenced. With the re-introduction of the West Yorkshire League and formation of several new competitions – namely the Bradford Alliance & Bradford Combination Leagues – the Bradford & District League was reduced to two sections for the 1902-03 season. However, a number of more 'informal' teams were still playing friendly, or 'ordinary' fixtures – and surprisingly the name of Bradford City was among these.

There had been no reports of the demise of the previous 'Bradford City' in the local press – in an age when Rugby was still the dominant winter game in the region, and therefore it is no surprise that the 'new' club should receive any attention either.

There is little to suggest that this is the same club as that which played so successfully the previous season. There were no match reports involving the club and certainly no information as to where matches were played, however their results did appear from time to time in Saturday evening 'Football Special' editions of the 'Bradford Daily Argus'.

With many of the 'Football Specials' missing, those listed below can in no way be perceived as being a complete list of results. However, those matches that have been traced all seem to have ended in victories for the City side !

The first mention of the 'new' Bradford City was the result of their *reserve* team's 2-1 victory over Rutland Street Albion. Absolutely nothing else is known about this match!

Bradford City's first team were then known to have played Fieldhead Albion at home (20/9/1902) and then away (27/9/1902). Neither result is known although the team for the former game was:

      Taylor (goal), **Horsfall, Milnes** (backs), **Piggin, Wilson, Aldersley** (half backs), **Smithies** *captain*, **Blaythorn, Watson, Illingworth, Northing** (forwards).

Clearly this is not the same side as that from twelve months earlier. A side called Kingswood was then known to have been defeated on 4th October, by 2-1, the side that day being somewhat different:

Knowles (goal), **Tolman, Furness** (backs), **Horsfall, Smithies, Blaythorn** (half backs), **Castor, Illingworth, Clapham, Taylor, Watson** (forwards),

One week later the 'Bradford Daily Argus' carried TWO results for Bradford City – a 2-0 defeat of Bowling Juniors & a 3-0 victory against Villa Rangers. No doubt one of these victorious sides was the aforementioned reserve side.

Wilsden United were over-run by the tune of 11-1 on October 18th 1902, followed by St.Augustines seven days later who went down 7-0 to the rampant City side. There is then no more mention of Bradford City until their victory over Leeds Road United on 7th MARCH 1903. City hit 11 that day and were never mentioned again !

Obviously this was a much more informal City side who possibly played in much more rudimentary surroundings than their predecessors and those that followed. It is extremely doubtful whether Greenfield was used - there was a Greenfield Albion playing competitively by now, possibly using the ground in the absence of the previous incumbents. What is clear is that this side have an even more obscure history than any other Bradford City in history !

Furthermore, all of City's opponents from the 1902-03 season also faded into obscurity over the following few months, underlining the informal nature of clubs playing ' ordinary' fixtures at this time.

By the time of the victory over Leeds Road United, Manningham Rugby club's plans to become the new professional Bradford City were actually well underway. The rest, as they say, is history.......

One interesting item from the 1902-03 season was Valley Parade's *first* fire. It occurred during a District Cup semi-final between St.Cuthberts and Rawdon when a bale of hay somehow ignited. Luckily no-one was harmed and it was described by many as being far more exciting than the cup tie itself !

5
CLUB COLOURS

The subject of club colours leads to many problems as regards both Bradford FC and the original Bradford City clubs. The local press of the time gave match reports, and details as to where local sides of that time played, but there was no reference to the colours adopted by the local amateurs.

At the time of Bradford rugby club's first serious flirtation with the round ball game the rugby section took to the field in red, amber and black hoops. These were the original colours worn by Bradford cricket club, formed in 1836 and who had merged with Bradford rugby club in 1880. It is more than likely therefore that the association section of the club also adopted these colours between the years of 1895 & 1899. It is no coincidence that three of the city's senior football clubs – Bradford (Park Avenue), Bradford RUFC (now merged with Bingley sports club) and Bradford Northern/Bulls RLFC - have all used red, amber and black kits at one time or another, as they are all descended from the original Bradford rugby club that graced Park Avenue.

It has been suggested that the colours of red, amber and black were in fact the colours associated with Bradford before the granting of it's coat of arms and certainly before it's city status, given in 1897.

It has not been possible to correctly identify the club colours worn by either of the first two Bradford City clubs though. Whereas the current Bradford City adopted the claret and amber of Manningham rugby club upon their inception to the Football League in 1903, it is almost certain that the earlier sides of the same name were totally unrelated clubs and as such used completely different 'kits' to that of the current Bradford City FC. With the second, and most obscure amateur Bradford City side playing only friendly fixtures during the 1902-03 season it is possible that a more informal type of playing kit was used anyway. It was not unheard of for sides to take the field in normal 'workwear', particularly if that side was playing on an informal basis only, or maybe because they were too impoverished to purchase a set of football jerseys. It has to be remembered that these were the days in which a set of wooden posts would be placed in a field, maybe sawdust or chalk used to draw lines, and a game rather different to the one we know these days played. There was no hint of goal-nets or hot running water – a nearby stream would do if you were lucky. 'Crude' or informal friendlies were not uncommon, and it is in this climate at the turn of the 20th century that the second Bradford City club certainly existed.

The reason for Manningham rugby club's adoption of claret and amber is still unclear. Formed in 1880, possible as successors to the old Manningham Albion club, Manningham originally played in black shirts and white shorts, before settling for the claret and amber alternative for the first time on 20th September 1884 against Hull at Carlisle Road. Various ideas have been put forward for this choice of colours: that they had a military origin, linked to the nearby Belle Vue barracks; or that they were adopted to signify the view held in Australia at that time that the colours of claret and amber represented 'blood & mustard' – a metaphor for the fighting qualities of blood and strength ?

In any case the colours adopted by Manningham were certainly distinctive – Bradford City remain the only professional soccer club in England to wear them.

THE FIRST 'BANTAMS' !

The nickname of the current Bradford City is of course, 'The Bantams', due to the apparent resemblance of the teams colours to the plumage of bantams (they have also been known as 'The Paraders' & 'The Citizens', while Manningham rugby club were at one time nicknamed 'The Wasps', with their claret and amber hoops).

There was in fact an earlier team known as 'The Bantams' – a side that was totally unrelated to Bradford City in every way !

South London side West Norwood FC were formed in 1885, originally known as Stanley FC & Novices FC, they had worked their way up to the famous Spartan League by 1907, and even more renown Isthmian League by the 1920's via a number of local leagues. Without going into too much detail regarding a far flung team some 200 miles from Bradford itself, West Norwood were from 1894 known as 'The Bantams'. This was due to the small stature of their players and, as far as I can ascertain, had nothing to do with the colours the team adorned !

Many thanks to John Dewhirst & Pete Zemroch for much of the information on club colours relating to Bradford and Manningham rugby clubs. For further information on club colours, and on the current Bradford City's 'Bantams' nickname, the City Gent website can provide a detailed commentary.
www.TheCityGent.com

6
GREENFIELD

Greenfield can be regarded as one of Bradford's many 'lost' sports grounds. Located along the northern side of Cutler Heights Lane, close to its junction with Sticker Lane, the area is now used as industrial units after having been demolished, like much of old Dudley Hill, to make way for part of the road widening scheme in the area.

It had first been used many years before the formation of the original Bradford City FC, and certainly as a rugby (and possibly soccer) ground as indicated by the presence of the now long-gone Bowling FC fixture list from Yorkshire Rugby Union's 1883-84 handbook.

A Greenfield 'association' side played in the Bradford & District Cup in the 1899-1900 season, indicating that soccer was still being played there as well as rugby before Bradford City arrived on the scene. Certainly after City's demise, local cup games were played there, and by around 1909 Sunfield Rovers had moved from the Tong Street area to play on the ground in the Bradford & District League. It is highly likely that other clubs used the ground in the interim and afterwards, facilities at this time being very basic – there were after all several teams through the years using the 'Greenfield' name, most notably Greenfield Athletic FC who were among the founder members of the West Riding County Amateur League.

In preparation for the professional Bradford City's first season in division one, Valley Parade underwent major surgery, prompting the professional side to make use of Greenfield for two practice matches in the summer of 1908. Both games saw City players divided into two teams – the first, on the evening of Saturday August 8th raised over £40 for the Bradford Hospitals trust as over 6,000 spectators chose to attend. The second game, played in atrocious weather conditions raised only £7 10s as 1,000 were in attendance.

Bradford Northern played their first season – 1907-08 – at Greenfield. They paid £8 to Whitakers Brewery (who became the club's match sponsors), before moving to Bowling Old Lane's current cricket ground on Birch Lane. Fans had complained that a trek out to Greenfield was too far and as a result overall attendances were disappointing, only 7,000 turning out for the first game against Huddersfield. Northern, formed after the original Bradford northern union (Rugby League) club's decision to introduce professional soccer to Park

Avenue, actually took their grandstand with them when they moved from Greenfield after having spent £302 on that, fencing and the pitch in their short tenure there. Ironically, Bowling Old Lane had 12 months earlier refused Northern's offer of £50 rent for the ground before the club's decision to rent Greenfield.

The Greenfield ground was described as a six acre field, with a pear shaped running and trotting track around it. In fact, it was officially known as the 'Yorkshire Trotting & Athletic Grounds' in the 1920's, becoming a Greyhound Stadium in 1927. The first competitive racing commenced on October 8th of that year, when a crowd of 13,000 witnessed the proceedings. Financially strapped Bradford Northern almost moved back to the site in 1929, which by now had cover for 20,000, but were thwarted when they failed to raise the £700 necessary as their share of upgrading the ground.

In it's heyday, Greenfield had two wooden covered sides, the main stand located on the Cutler Heights Lane side of the ground. Opposite was the smaller barrelled-roofed School Street stand on the railway side. Black and white painted barge boards were seen to adorn the covered parts of the ground. The Board Street side of the ground had a tall tote board, surrounded by a flat, relatively unused, standing area. Opposite this there was a high raised terrace which saw the crowd raised above the dogs.

The Bradford & District Motor Club introduced dirt track racing –a version of speedway – to Greenfield in 1928. However, racing at the 'Greenfield Autodrome' realised poor attendances and after only four meets the venture was abandoned. However, August 1961 saw motorcycle racing return to the track in the form of Bradford Panthers Speedway team. The Panthers had been formed two years earlier and had experienced a successful two years at Odsal before their short move to Greenfield. The team did not last, hosting their final home fixture in the Provincial League in October 1962 before folding soon after.

The nearby Greenfield Hotel, which had served as a base for sides such as Bowling FC over the years, was demolished along with the ground in the 1960's to make way for the new industrial warehousing. After the third race at the greyhound meetings, spectators were able to get a 'pass-out' in order to acquire drinks there.

BOWLING F.C.

First Team.	Second Team.
Oct. 6 Denfield, home	Denfield, away
13 Buttershaw Mills, away	Buttershaw Mills, home
20	Scholes Albert Mills, home
27 Leeds East End, away	Leeds East End, home
Nov. 3 Brighouse, home	Brighouse, away
10 Alverthorpe Rangers, away	Allerton Rangers, home
17 Gildersome, home	Gildersome, away
24 Bradford Rangers, home	Bradford Rangers, away
Dec. 1 Otley, away	Otley, home
8 Leeds East End, home	Leeds East End, away
15 Denfield, away	Denfield, home
22 Castleford, home	Scholes Albert Mills, away
29 Brighouse, away	Brighouse, home
Jan. 5 Buttershaw Mills, home	Buttershaw Mills, away
12 Holbeck, home	Holbeck, away
19 Stanley, away	Howden Clough, home
26 Alverthorpe Rangers, home	Howden Clough, away
Feb. 2 Stanley, home	Hartshead Moor, away
9 Castleford, away	Hartshead Moor, home
16 Scholes, home	Allerton Rangers, away
23 Gildersome, away	Gildersome, home
March 1 (Cup Tie)Dodworth, a	Bowling Wanderers, away
8 Bradford Rangers, away	Bradford Rangers, home
15 Church Hill, away	Church Hill, home
22 Otley, home	Otley, away
29 Holbeck, away	Holbeck, home
April 5 Church Hill, home	Church Hill, away
12 Scholes, away	Bowling Wanderers, home

Hon. Sec.—Mr. G.W. Ingle, 36 Hall Lane, Bradford
Captains—1st, Mr. James Wright; 2nd, Mr. L. Booth
Head-quarters and Dressing-room—Greenfield Hotel,
Dudley Hill
Ground—Adjoining Greenfield Hotel; two minutes' walk
from Dudley Hill Station (G.N.)
Club colours—Navy Blue, with White Maltese Cross

35

*One of the first sides to play at **Greenfield** were Bowling Rugby Club, their
fixtures & opponents in 1883-84 make interesting reading. Among their rivals
were Church Hill, whose 'association' side were later to become opponents of
the first Bradford City FC.*

PAID WITH THANKS.

The Parrs Wood Press

SPORTS PUBLISHING AND REPORTING SERVICES

St Wilfrid's Enterprise Centre, Royce Road, Manchester M15 5BJ

Tel/Fax: *0161 226 4466*

Email: sport@parrswoodpress.com

Website: www.parrswoodpress.com

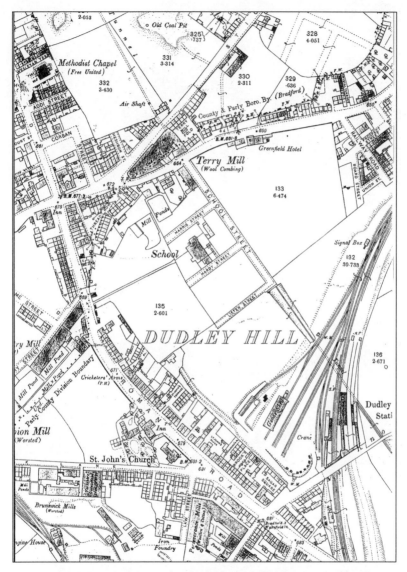

*Pre-Bradford City **Greenfield – 1893.** No doubt the field at this time had little in
the way of what can be called facilities. During these times local sides would, upon
paying rent or similar payment to the land-owners, bring goal (or rugby) posts
with them, mark out the pitch with sawdust or something similar, then simply up-
sticks at the end of the game and retire to the hotel for liquid refreshment.*

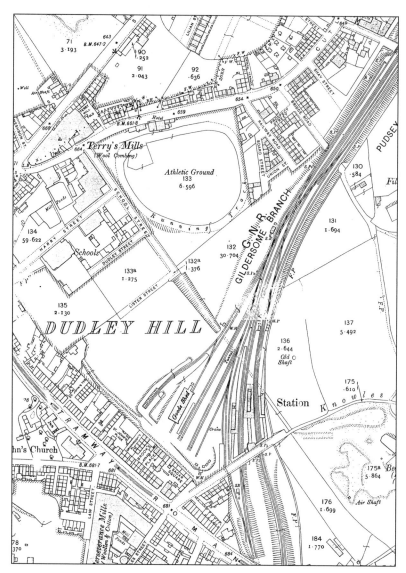

*Post-Bradford City **Greenfield - 1908**. By now the area is officially defined as an 'athletic ground', complete with 'running' track. Note the ground's proximity to the old Dudley Hill station. Much of the Dudley Hill area around the old cross-roads was flattened to make way for the road-widening scheme in the area in the 1960's.*

Greenfield Stadium. *This photograph was taken just before its demise.*

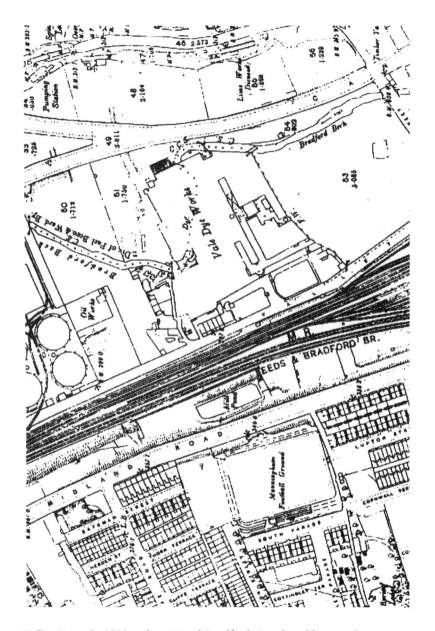

Valley Parade 1893 – *the original Bradford City played here as the away team in the 1901-02 season*

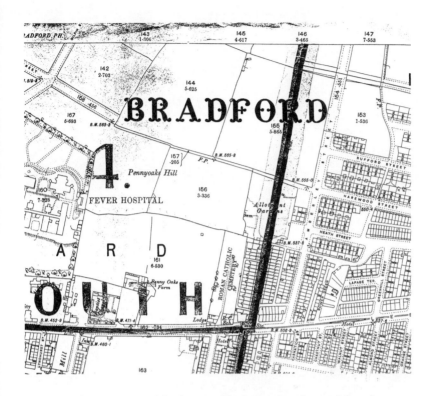

Harewood Street – 1893. The first Bradford City played one of their first ever competitive fixtures here against the home side, Church Hill. Harewood Street lies off Barkerend Road, and just to the north of the old Leeds Road Hospital. It is likely that Church Hill played in one of the fields marked 144 or 155. The area is now covered with terraced housing. There is a recreation ground still in use as a sports field to the left of the old hospital, although it is unlikely to be that used by Church Hill. It is also possible that Harewood Recreation FC's Boldshay Fields ground was in the vicinity.

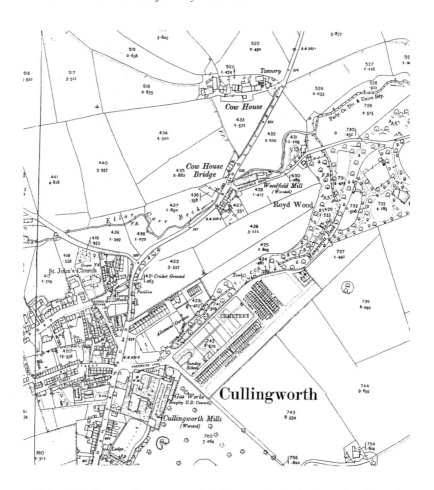

This old Ordnance Survey map of Cullingworth clearly shows Royd Wood, which was said to be the location of the old Cullingworth FC ground around 1901. Bradford City played their first ever competitive fixture on this ground, which could well have been at, or close to, the current cricket ground, which is also shown on the map.

7
...AND THE LADIES

Although in no way related to Bradford City or Bradford FC (presumably), one of the first 'association' sides in the city was a ladies team !

Whereas the local press made little reference to the round ball game – in the absence of any organised teams in the district – there was some reference to an un-named women's team in 1895.

Where the 'practice ground', mentioned in the following two reports was, and whether they fulfilled any proper fixtures is unknown, but the following excerpts from the 'Bradford Daily Argus' – Saturday 25th January 1895 – just about sum up the view of womens football held at that time (the poem obviously refers to the rugby code !) .

There is nothing to suggest that the team stayed together for very long, for I have been unable to locate any further reference to them in any of the local newspapers of the day. In any case, this particular experiment was obviously considered something of a novelty, judging by the tone of the reports. Equality was certainly a way off, the women not considered well enough built to play in the mud, and 'charging' eliminated from their game – 'charging' being an accepted part of the game in this day and age. Neither was it considered good for the complexion of the fairer sex – how things have changed !

and will have some difficulty in getting teams.

LADIES AT FOOTBALL.

A football correspondent of a London evening contemporary says he went to see the practice of the lady footballers the other afternoon, but only about a dozen turned up, and the ground was in such a horrible condition as to disarm criticism. This is how he describes the amazons, who are, of course, Association players. They are a bright and enthusiastic lot these fair footballers, but to see them floundering through a sea of slush was not pleasant, though the scene was evidently jolly for those spectators who had perched themselves upon the fencing. There was a regular hurricane blowing, but anyhow the kicking is not hard enough, though the shooting at goal was singularly accurate. Miss Honeyball, who was indisposed, sat up in the Press-box and gave advice more or less accepted. Whether the scheme prove a success or no, there is evidently a deal of talent among the team, and personally I was considerably surprised by the good form of one lady in white, who dribbled down and kicked with the style of a Corinthian. Others there are who show no tact, especially in passing, but I expect a great impro ..ent to be effected all round by the time the first match takes place. The ladies generally made an artistic picture in their variegated colours, and seemed to heartily enter into the spirit of the thing. But ladies are not built to play in the mud. I wonder how it would look if a League secretary came on the ground and kissed all the players with affectionate welcome !"

FOOTBALL IN FRANCE

FOOTBALL FOR LADIES.

The Ladies' Football Club, to which one may wish better fortune than befel the team of profession cricketers of the same sex, have been defeated——we make haste to add by the weather. They are said to have shown of late a disinclination, with which it is easy to sympathise, to practice in the cold, to say nothing of the mud, from which it may be inferred that the ladies are not such sticklers for "the rigour of the game" as was Sarah Battle at her whist. The few, hardier than the rest, who have continued to play in the snow and rain—without umbrellas, too—deserve no less pity than admiration. With no intention of underrating the courage of these gallant ladies, it must be pointed out that although football undoubtedly develops the muscles, it is not good for the complexion under certain conditions, and the rules of the game do not favour elegance in dress—which things are not to be despised. A wit has suggested that football matches should be settled " by arbitration," but the ladies will no doubt teach us how the game may be played without danger—or excitement.

POINTS.

A Boston girl is supposed to have written this graphic and illuminating description of football, as seen by feminine eyes :—

First came some men all dressed in blue,
  Then others came in red,
One fellow yelled, the rest all tried
  To jump upon his head.

And then another fellow yelled,
  And each man, where he stood,
Just hit, and struck, and knocked and kicked,
  At every one he could.

And then one fell upon his neck,
  And all the others ran,
And on his prone and prostrate form
  Leaped every blessed man.

And then the ambulance drove on,
  And, loaded up with men
With twisted necks and broken lungs,
  Went driving off again.

The football match with women players will be played according to Association rules, but the roughness will be eliminated by prohibiting charging. The ball is also to be smaller than the one used by men. It it understood that the players are now being coached.

8
BRADFORD AMATEUR LEAGUES –
..............THE BEGINNING

With the Bradford & District Football Association being formed in March 1899, it was obvious that a local senior league would follow. It is interesting to see from the following league tables and lists which clubs were around at the time. Several sides, such as those in the old West Yorkshire & Yorkshire Leagues were 'association' sections of Northern Union (Rugby league) clubs, and many were formed by those completely new to the round ball game which had taken far too long to establish itself in the West Riding. Local churches were among the first to jump on the 'bandwagon', organising teams as a way of increasing their congregation and of furthering the values of good health, this had already been achieved successfully with the growth in popularity of cricket in the summer months.

A season-by-season look at the constitution of Bradford's earliest leagues illustrates clearly not only the growth in popularity of the game, but the fluidity of membership of these early organisations as 'young' men experimented with the round ball game for the first time. This is by no means meant to be a full history of the early Bradford 'association' leagues, just an overview of which teams took part in the early seasons of Bradford's soccer history.

1898-99

Prior to the formation of the local FA, a Bradford 'Junior' League was in operation, containing eight clubs. It is unclear whether the 'junior' status applied to the playing status of the clubs concerned or whether there was an upper-age limit for players.

In an exciting finish to the season, Church Hill Crescent defeated Bradford Wanderers 2-1 in their final fixture to force a play-off for the title. Wanderers gained revenge when they won the deciding match 1-0 in front of 800 spectators at Valley Parade to take the championship.

```
┌─────────────────────────────────────────────────────────────┐
│        BRADFORD JUNIOR LEAGUE - FINAL TABLE 1898-99           │
```

	P	W	L	D	F	A	Pts
Church Hill Cres.	14	11	2	1	53	17	23
Bradford Wndrs	14	11	2	1	48	14	23
St.Judes	14	7	6	1	27	25	15
Park View	14	6	5	3	42	38	15
Sedgefield Rov.	14	7	7	0	40	35	14
West View	14	5	8	3	37	37	13
Moorlands Utd	14	4	9	1	26	41	9
Frizinghall Jnrs	14	0	14	0	17	73	0

Bradford Wanderers won play off against Church Hill Crescent.

1899-1900

The first Bradford & District League champions were Girlington, who, as a result of their large following, and had to resort to playing home games at the nearby Valley Parade enclosure to accommodate their supporters. Airedale & Rawdon were Girlington's nearest challengers The top local clubs were certainly not short of players, many of them already running reserve sides in the league's second division. Divisions 2A & 2B contained many of those teams who had competed in the Bradford Junior League the previous season.

Rawdon defeated Girlington 2-0 to become the first ever District Cup winners, in a game played at Valley Parade (this after a scoreless draw at the same venue).

BRADFORD & DISTRICT LEAGUE – DIV. 1 FINAL TABLE **1899-1900**

	P	W	D	L	F	A	Pts
Girlington	20	17	0	3	67	11	37
Airedale	20	13	3	4	64	9	30
Rawdon	20	12	3	5	46	17	29
Cullingworth	20	11	4	5	46	28	27
Park Chapel	20	8	7	6	26	43	22
Clayton	20	8	9	3	24	37	19
St.Andrews	20	6	9	5	24	39	17
Harewood Rec.	20	6	9	5	38	38	15
Ilkley	20	3	12	5	17	37	11
Bradford Trinity	20	1	15	4	15	41	6
Belgrave	20	2	16	2	16	79	6

Nb…Harewood 2 points deducted, Bradford Trinity withdrew before the end of the season, points awarded to opponents in unplayed fixtures. Goals for & against do not tally.

DIVISION 2A
Park View
St.Judes
Church Hill
Sedgefield Rovers
Airedale (reserves)
Girlington (reserves)
St.Andrews (reserves)
Clayton (reserves)

DIVISION 2B
Wesley Place
Bedford Trinity
Frizinghall Juniors
Greenfield
West View
Moorlands
Midland Rovers
St.Columbas Athletic
Sedgefield Rovers (reserves)

1900-01

The Bradford & District League gained Menston, Otley & Keighley from the West Yorkshire League, although the latter side (the first from the town to play properly organised games) disbanded before the season's end. Girlington were league champions for the second time but went down to Rawdon again in the District Cup final – this time the score was 4-2 in a final, again played at Valley Parade.

A Manningham & District League was formed for this season, Shipley winning the title in a championship race that went right to the wire. There were also several Manningham-based sides in the much stronger Bradford & District League – although ironically it was the side from Girlington that played on the well established Valley Parade ground in the township.

BRADFORD & DISTRICT LEAGUE 1900-01

DIVISION 1	DIVISION 2	DIVISION 3
Girlington	Church Hill	Greenfield
Rawdon	Great Horton	Bedford Trinity
Airedale	Menston Clarence	Frizinghall
Otley	Park View	Hallfield Baptists
Cullingworth	St.Judes	Manningham St.Marks
Menston	Sedgefield Rovers	Manningham St.Pauls
Harewood Recreation	Airedale (reserves)	Birkenshaw St.Pauls
Clayton	St.Andrews (reserves)	Moorlands
Belgrave	Girlington (reserves)	Park View (reserves)
St.Andrews	Harewood Rec. (reserves)	Sedgefield Rov (reserves)
Keighley w/d	Clayton (reserves)	

MANNINGHAM & DISTRICT LEAGUE – FINAL TABLE **1900-01**

	P	**W**	**L**	**D**	**Pts**
Shipley	14	9	3	2	20
Four Lane Ends	14	7	2	5	19
Church Hill (reserves)	14	8	4	2	18
Girlington Shamrocks	13	6	2	5	17
Manningham Wanderers	12	7	4	1	15
Girlington Congregational	11	3	3	5	11
Bradford St.Marys	12	1	11	0	2
Manningham St.Pauls (res)	11	0	11	0	0

Not all teams completed their fixtures – but this was considered 'final'. Goals for and against columns were never printed for this league.

1901-02

Menston returned to the West Yorkshire League, but they were replaced by BRADFORD CITY. Airedale were of course league champions, closely followed by City, while Girlington at last won the District Cup 2-1 at Airedale's expense.

The Bradford & District League had by now quickly grown to four divisions, absorbing the former Manningham League clubs into it's bottom two sections., although there were certainly enough clubs in that particular district to have formed a separate league!

Despite a good deal of research, there appear to be no final tables published for this historic season.

BRADFORD & DISTRICT LEAGUE 1901-02

DIVISION 1	DIVISION 2	DIVISION 3
Airedale	St.Judes	Shipley
Bradford City	Swaine Hill United	Harewood Recreation
Girlington	Eccleshill	Frizinghall
Otley	Great Horton	Girlington Shamrocks
Church Hill	Sedgefield Rovers	Hallfield Baptists
Clayton	Park View	Manningham St.Pauls
Cullingworth	West View	Manningham St.Marks
Rawdon	Birkenshaw St.Pauls	Manningham Rangers
Belgrave w/d	Menston (reserves)	Manningham Athletic
	Airedale (reserves)	Thornbury
	Girlington (reserves)	Otley (reserves)
	Bedford Trinity w/d	Sedgefield Rov (reserves)
		Rawdon (reserves)

DIVISION 4		
Bradford Pin Company	Four Lane Ends	Bedford Trinity (reserves)
Brownroyd	West Bowling	St.Judes (reserves)
Bradford Rovers	Barkerend	Eccleshill (reserves)
Bankfoot St.Matthews	Bramley Street Mission	Church Hill (reserves)
St.Cuthberts	Manningham St.Pauls (res)	

1902-03

The Bradford & District League was decimated when Airedale & Rawdon joined the West Yorkshire League. Girlington were also to join that league but surprisingly disbanded instead, along with Bradford City. Menston rejoined the local league, but there were only two divisions this season.

There were many more organised teams in the city however – the formation of the Bradford Combination and Alliance leagues being a consequence of this. The District League was clearly the strongest, followed by the Alliance (champions were Guiseley Celtic) and then the Combination, which was considered the weakest of the three leagues. A Bradford Schools League was by now also in existence.

Rawdon defeated improving St.Cuthberts 2-0 in the District Cup final, while Church Hill were Bradford & District League champions for the first and only time. They were convincing winners, winning 16 and drawing 1 of their 18 fixtures (65 goals scored, 14 conceded). Again, due to the onset of the cricket season, the local press quickly turned it's back on local soccer – and as a result final tables were not published (although not all teams will have completed their fixtures).

BRADFORD & DISTRICT LEAGUE 1902-03

DIVISION 1	DIVISION 2
Airedale (reserves)	Four Lane Ends
Otley	St.Cuthberts
Cullingworth	Manningham St.Pauls
Menston	Manningham St.Marks
Park View	Manningham Rangers
St.Judes w/d	White Abbey Wesleyans
Oakenshaw	Greenfield
Church Hill	Wyke Parish Church
Sedgefield	
Swaine Hill United	
Great Horton w/d	
Eccleshill	

BRADFORD & DISTRICT ALLIANCE 1902-03

DIVISION 1	DIVISION 2	DIVISION 3
Guiseley Celtic	Dalcross	Holme Lane
Southend Wesleyans	Bramley St.Mission	Bradford Rovers
Greengates	Bowling	Idle Parish Church
Bradford Pin Company	All Saints	Bedford Trinity
Thornton	West Bowling	Bierley
Queensbury	Springfield Athletic	Eccleshill Rovers
Guiseley New Scarborough	Manningham Clarence	City United
Heaton	Manningham Recreation	Villa United
Girlington Shamrocks w/d	Thornbury	Bowling (reserves)
Great Horton (reserves) w/d	Wyke Parish Church (res)	Manningham Rec. (res)
Eccleshill (reserves)	Oakenshaw (reserves)	
Swaine Hill United (reserves)		

BRADFORD & DISTRICT COMBINATION
1902-03

DIVISION 1	DIVISION 2
Bowling Athletic	Bradford Celtic
Parkside Crescent	College Road
Croft & Perkins	Bankfoot Rovers
Horton Rovers	Church Hill Wanderers
Laisterdyke Albion	Lister Hills
Boldshay	Birch Lane
Parish Church	Undercliffe Rovers
Daisy Hill	Bowbridge
St.Oswalds	Whetley United
Victor Albion	Westfield
Prospect	
St.Columbas	
Girlington United	

1903-04

Among the new faces in the Bradford & District League's top division were Bingley, plus Bradford Combination champions Guiseley Celtic. All the three leagues were decimated by withdrawals, many games were left unplayed, and the Bradford & District League first division title race ended in controversy. Menston were awarded 4 points for unplayed games against St.Judes at the season's close, lifting them 2 points ahead of the Guiseley side, who were rightfully aggrieved, having led the table based on games played. Despite appeals to the league, Menston were thus awarded the league title.

The Bradford Combination's top division saw only six sides complete the season, as several sides dropped out. The most notable withdrawals however were previous season's Bradford & District League champions and founder members of the league, Church Hill, who resigned in March.

St.Cuthberts, who had now risen from division four to division one of the Bradford & District League, defeated Menston 2-1 in the District Cup final, thus depriving their rivals of a league and cup double.

By now, most areas of Bradford had soccer teams representing them. They, along with the many church-based teams, made up the 80 or so playing in local league. There were still other sides around the city playing only friendly fixtures.

BRADFORD & DISTRICT LEAGUE   1903-04

DIVISION 1	DIVISION 2
Menston	Manningham Rangers
Guiseley Celtic	Manningham Recreation
St.Cuthberts	Manningham St.Marks w/d
Park View	Harewood Recreation
Oakenshaw w/d	Bramley Street Mission
St.Judes	Guiseley New Scarborough
Sedgefield w/d	Bedford Trinity w/d
Church Hill w/d	Holme Lane
Swaine Hill United	Thornton
Otley	White Abbey Wesleyans
Bingley	Greenfield
Four Lane Ends	Technical College
	Birkenshaw w/d

BRADFORD & DISTRICT ALLIANCE 1903-04

DIVISION 1	DIVISION 2	DIVISION 3
Dalcross	Bowling Juniors	Parish Church
Bradford Rovers	Thornbury	Greenfield Albion
Laisterdyke Albion	Salroyd	Nethertown
Rawdon United	Villa United	Dudley Hill
Heaton	Idle St.George	Prospect
Bierley	Eccleshill Rovers	Horton Rovers
Boldshay	City United w/d	Birkenshaw St.Pauls
Eccleshill	Church Hill (reserves)	St.Bartholemews w/d
Henshaw St.Johns	Manningham St.Marks (res)	Gildersome Parish Church
Menston Clarence	Oakenshaw (reserves)	
Bankfoot St.Matthews	Guiseley Celtic (reserves)	
Manningham Rec (res) w/d		

BRADFORD & DISTRICT COMBINATION 1903-04

DIVISION 1	DIVISION 2	DIVISION 3
Bradford St.Johns	Greengates St.Johns	Bolton United
Bradford Celtic	St.Patricks	St.Leonards
Low Moor Hotspurs	Bowling White Star	Westfield Rovers
Brunswick Albion	Tanner Hill	Eccleshill United
Ingleby United	Kingswood	Otley Road Mission
Gardeners	Bradford St.Marys	Longside Recs
Undercliffe Rovers w/d	Rawdon Juniors	St.Augustines
St.Michaels w/d	Salem Athletic	Oakenshaw Juniors
	Allerton	Rawdon Recreation (res)
	J.Shaw & Co	Bfd St.Johns (reserves)
	St.Judes (reserves)	
	Laisterdyke Albion (reserves)	

.....in later years we would see the birth of the famous old 'Bradford Amateur' and 'Bradford Nig-Nog' leagues, as well as the relatively short-lived 'Bradford Industrial League', and the 'Bradford Red Triangle League', which is still in existence as the Grattan League. Slightly further way, the Keighley & District League ran from 1905-1963, and at the time of its demise was one of the county's longest surviving leagues. Even further into the future, the 1960's & 1970's saw the birth of Sunday league soccer and a proliferation of new leagues in and around Bradford.

9
1895-96 & 1901-02 SEASONS

The West Riding lagged behind the rest of the country as far as the 'association' game was concerned. The top Midlands & North-Western sides had formed the Football League in 1888, and the FA Cup was a well established competition among sides from virtually all parts of the country, including southern Yorkshire. The West Riding could offer token representatives in the competition, Bradford (as previously mentioned), Hunslet, and Mirfield United amongst others finding success relatively hard to come by. Northern Union – today's present day Rugby League - ruled supreme, the top clubs from the north of England breaking away from the south-dominated Rugby Union in 1895 to form their own competition.

For the record, these were the outcomes of other competitions during the 1895-1896 (the season of Bradford FC's first, successful, attempt at the round ball game) and 1901-02 (the first Bradford City's only campaign) seasons:

1895-96

ASSOCIATION FOOTBALL

FOOTBALL LEAGUE: Division 1							
	P	**W**	**D**	**L**	**F**	**A**	**Pts**
Aston Villa	30	20	5	5	78	45	45
Derby County	30	17	7	6	68	35	41
Everton	30	16	7	7	66	43	39
Bolton Wanderers	30	16	5	9	49	37	37
Sunderland	30	15	7	8	52	41	37
Stoke	30	15	0	15	56	47	30
The Wednesday	30	12	5	13	44	53	29
Blackburn Rovers	30	12	5	13	40	50	29
Preston North End	30	11	6	13	44	48	28
Burnley	30	10	7	13	48	44	27
Bury	30	12	3	15	50	54	27
Sheffield United	30	10	6	14	40	50	26
Nottingham Forest	30	11	3	16	42	57	25
Wolverhampton W	30	10	1	19	61	65	21
Small Heath	30	8	4	18	39	79	20
West Bromwich Alb	30	6	7	17	30	59	19

FOOTBALL LEAGUE DIVISION 2: Liverpool, r/u: Manchester City
F.A. CUP: Final: The Wednesday...2   Wolverhampton Wanderers...1
    (at Crystal Palace)
F.A. AMATEUR CUP: Final: Bishop Auckland...1   RA Portsmouth...0
    (at Leicester)
NORTHERN LEAGUE: Darlington, r/u: South Bank
MIDLAND LEAGUE: Kettering, r/u: Gainsborough Trinity
WEST YORKSHIRE LEAGUE: joint champions: Hunslet & **Bradford**
LEEDS WORKPEOPLES HOSPITAL CUP: Final: **Bradford**...4
       Featherstone...1 (after 1-1 draw) both games played at Kirkstall

NORTHERN UNION

NORTHERN RUGBY LEAGUE CHAMPIONSHIP:							
	P	**W**	**D**	**L**	**F**	**A**	**Pts**
Manningham	42	33	0	9	367	158	66
Halifax	42	30	5	7	312	139	65
Runcorn	42	24	8	10	314	143	56
Oldham	42	27	2	13	374	194	56
Brighouse Rangers	42	22	9	11	247	129	53
Tyldesley	42	21	8	13	260	164	50
Hunslet	42	24	2	16	279	207	50
Hull	42	23	3	16	259	158	49
Leigh	42	21	4	17	214	269	46
Wigan	42	19	7	16	245	147	45
Bradford	42	18	9	15	254	175	45
Leeds	42	20	3	19	258	247	43
Warrington	42	17	5	20	198	240	39
St.Helens (-2pts)	42	15	8	19	195	230	36
Liversedge	42	15	4	23	261	355	34
Widnes	42	14	4	24	177	323	32
Stockport	42	12	8	22	171	315	32
Batley	42	12	7	23	137	298	31
Wakefield Trinity	42	13	4	25	156	318	30
Huddersfield	42	10	4	28	194	274	24
Broughton Rangers	42	8	8	26	165	244	24
Rochdale Hornets	42	4	8	30	78	388	16

BRADFORD JUNIOR LEAGUE CLUBS	
Greenfield	Gilstead
Victoria Rangers (still in existence today !)	Pudsey
Bolton Woods	Cross Roads
Steeton	Worth Village
Keighley St.Annes	Keighley Clarence

RUGBY UNION
YORKSHIRE CUP: Final: Castleford...3 West Riding...0

1901-02

ASSOCIATION FOOTBALL

FOOTBALL LEAGUE: Division 1							
	P	**W**	**D**	**L**	**F**	**A**	**Pts**
Sunderland	34	19	6	9	50	35	44
Everton	34	17	7	10	53	35	41
Newcastle United	34	14	9	11	48	34	37
Blackburn Rovers	34	15	6	13	52	48	36
Nottingham Forest	34	13	9	12	43	43	35
Derby County	34	13	9	12	39	41	35
Bury	34	13	8	13	44	38	34
Aston Villa	34	13	8	13	42	40	34
The Wednesday	34	13	8	13	48	52	34
Sheffield United	34	13	7	14	53	48	33
Liverpool	34	10	12	12	42	38	32
Bolton Wanderers	34	12	8	14	51	56	32
Notts. County	34	14	4	16	51	57	32
Wolverhampton W	34	13	6	15	46	57	32
Grimsby Town	34	13	6	15	44	60	32
Stoke	34	11	9	14	45	55	31
Small Heath	34	11	8	15	47	45	30
Manchester City	34	11	6	17	42	58	28

Nb...Small Heath now known as Birmingham City, Stoke now known as Stoke City, The Wednesday now Sheffield Wednesday.

FOOTBALL LEAGUE DIVISION 2: West Bromwich Alb, r/u: Middlesbrough
F.A. CUP: Final: Sheffield United (division 1)...2 Southampton (Southern
       Lge)...1 (after 1-1 draw) at Crystal Palace
F.A. AMATEUR CUP: Final: Old Malvernians...5 Bishop Auckland..1(at Leeds)
NORTHERN LEAGUE: Bishop Auckland, r/u: Grangetown Athletic
MIDLAND LEAGUE: Barnsley (reserves), r/u: Sheffield United (reserves)
SHEFFIELD ASSOCIATION LEAGUE: Barnsley ('A'), r/u: Denaby Utd
WEST YORKSHIRE CUP: Final: Altofts...4 Oulton St.Johns...1
BRADFORD & DISTRICT LEAGUE: Airedale, r/u: **Bradford City**
BRADFORD & DISTRICT F.A. CUP: Final: Girlington...2 Airedale...1
BRADFORD SCHOOLS CUP: Final: Belle Vue...3 Hanson...0
HUDDERSFIELD & DISTRICT LEAGUE: formed 1898, Shepley or Honley,
HUDDERSFIELD & DISTRICT F.A. CUP: Linthwaite Parish Church
HEAVY WOOLLEN WHEATLEY CUP: Final: Mirfield United...3 Savile
       Town Clarence...2
HALIFAX & DISTRICT CUP: Final: Lydgate...2 Whitehall...1

NORTHERN UNION

NORTHERN RUGBY LEAGUE CHAMPIONSHIP:						
	P	**W**	**D**	**L**	**F**	**A**	**Pts**
Broughton Rngrs	26	21	1	4	285	112	43
Salford	26	15	3	8	235	125	31
Runcorn	26	15	2	9	185	101	30
Swinton	26	16	0	10	226	121	28
Halifax	26	12	4	10	142	165	28
Bradford	26	14	1	11	201	157	27
Warrington	26	14	0	12	162	150	26
Hull	26	11	2	13	166	193	24
Oldham	26	10	2	14	190	169	22
Leigh	26	11	0	15	158	162	22
Hunslet	26	13	0	13	164	207	22
Batley	26	8	4	14	136	198	20
Huddersfield	26	8	2	16	122	262	18
Brighouse Rgrs	26	3	1	22	74	324	7

YORKSHIRE SENIOR COMPETITION: (as printed in the Keighley News)						
	P	**W**	**D**	**L**	**F**	**A**	**Pts**
Leeds	26	22	2	2	317	63	46
Manningham	26	19	1	6	212	85	37
Keighley	26	15	6	5	194	117	34
Wakefield Trinity	26	15	1	10	258	90	31
Holbeck	26	13	6	7	138	75	30
York	26	15	1	10	187	130	29
Normanton	26	13	2	11	148	140	28
Dewsbury	25	13	1	11	140	94	27
Castleford	25	9	3	13	115	142	21
Bramley	26	10	1	15	131	162	21
Heckmondwike	26	7	3	16	83	227	17
Goole	26	5	3	18	94	228	13
Sowerby Bridge	26	7	0	19	65	179	12
Liversedge	26	3	0	23	67	415	6

CHALLENGE CUP: Final: Broughton Rangers...25   Salford...0 (at Rochdale)

RUGBY UNION:
YORKSHIRE CUP: Final: Castleford...9   Old Dewsburians...6

OTHER SNIPPETS: April 1902 – Ibrox Park disaster, Glasgow, 25 killed & more than 500 injured when terracing collapsed. Newton Heath, 15th in division 2 of the Football League, change name to Manchester United.

10
BIBLIOGRAPHY

The Best of Bradford Amateur Football – Ronnie Wharton, 1987

A Pick of the Best of Bradford Amateur Football – Ronnie Wharton, 1989

The City Gent fanzine – various editions 1984-2000 (particularly David Pendleton's series on lost sports grounds of Bradford)

A Game That Would Pay- A Business History of Professional Football in Bradford – A.J.Arnold, 1988

The Origin & Development of Football in Leeds – Mike Green

City Memories – An Illustrated Record of Bradford City AFC – John Dewhirst, 1998

Bradford City: a Complete Record 1903-1988 – Terry Frost, 1988

The Grounds of Rugby League – Trevor Delaney, 1991

The Code War – Graham Williams, 1994

Glory Days – The History of English Rugby Union Cup Finals – Graham Williams, 1998

Images of Sport - Bradford Rugby League – Robert Gate, 2000

The F.A. Cup Complete Results – Tony Brown, 1999

Football League- Grounds For A Change – Dave Twydell, 1991

The Oldest Football Club in Bradford ? – Pete Zemroch (Bradford Park Avenue internet site), 2000

Soccer's Impact on the Northern Union in West Yorkshire 1895-1908, Trevor – Delaney, **in Code 13 Issue 9,** December 1988

Non League – Bob Barton, 1986

The Football League – Complete Tables 1888-1997, Yore Publications/Tony Brown, 1997

The Spartan Football League – Volume 1 1907-1930, Mike Wilson 2001

One Hundred Years of Local Football – A Short History of the Heavy Woollen District Football Association, Peter Hodgson, 1998

Chasing Glory - The Story of Association Football in Keighley, volume 1 – Rob Grillo, 1997

Glory Denied – The Story of Association Football in Keighley, volume 2 – Rob Grillo, 1999

Newspapers: Bradford Observer, Bradford Daily Telegraph, Bradford Daily Argus, Yorkshire Daily Observer, Keighley News, Shipley Times,

THE AUTHOR

Rob Grillo is currently Head of Geography at Greenhead High School, Keighley, West Yorkshire. Brought up in Keighley, he graduated from Loughborough University in the early 1990's. An ardent supporter of Bradford City FC, this is his fourth book, his previous efforts being on soccer and athletics in his home town.

A keen long-distance runner, Rob has also written extensively for local newspapers such as '*The Keighley News*' and Bradford '*Telegraph & Argus*', as well as several football-related magazines. He is a member of the Association of Sports Historians.

Also by Rob Grillo:

Chasing Glory - The Story of Association Football in Keighley, vol. 1, *1997*

Glory Denied – The Story of Association Football in Keighley, vol. 2, *1999*

Staying the Distance – The History of Distance Running in Keighley & District, *1999*